D1462018

TALKING BACK
TO THE
MEDIA

By
Peter Hannaford

Facts On File Publications
New York, New York ● Oxford, England

Dedicated to
HELEN KENNEDY ROGERS
My first boss; my first partner; a great teacher; a good friend

Talking Back to the Media

Library of Congress Cataloging in Publication Data

Hannaford, Peter.
  Talking back to the media.

  Includes index.
  1. Mass media—Audiences. 2. Public opinion.
I. Title.
P96.A83H36 1984   302.2'34'0973   83-8902
ISBN 0-87196-815-0

Printed in the United States of America
10 9 8 7 6 5 4 3 2 1

Composition by Facts On File/Circle Graphics
Printed by R.R. Donnelley & Sons, Co.

Contents

Acknowledgments

Many people from the worlds of business, politics, government and the media shared their experiences, perspectives and insights with me in the course of my writing this book. My special thanks go to the following: Kenneth Adelman, Richard V. Allen, John Bartolomeo, Lou Cannon, Jack Cox, M. Stanton Evans, Jim Foy, Donald Hannaford, Maureen Pater Hanson, Bruce Herschensohn, Max Hugel, Reed Irvine, Charles Ledgerwood, John McCarty, Robert McCloskey, Loye Miller, Jr., Anne Ready, Don Rothberg, Richard Salant, Herbert Schmertz, Larry Speakes, Robert Walker.

I owe thanks, too, to my wife, Irene, for her encouragement and her sharp typo-spotting eye as she read the manuscript.

Finally, my thanks go to my agent, Bill Adler, and his assistant, Julie Rosner, and to my editor, Philip Saltz, for their patience and guidance.

Peter D. Hannaford
Washington, D.C.
March 9, 1985

Part One
THE MEDIA
AND US

1/ Coming off the Media High

America's "Media High" is nearly over now. It lasted for more than a decade and affected the way we think about our institutions of government, business, the military, organized labor and religion. It also affected the institutions themselves. The worst effects of the Media High were cynicism, skepticism and national self-doubt.

The high itself was the product of disillusionment that grew out of the assassination of John F. Kennedy and our involvement in Vietnam. Watergate was the immediate trigger for it.

On June 19, 1972, the first story[1] by Robert Woodward and Carl Bernstein about the "third-rate burglary attempt" at the Democratic Party national headquarters on June 17 appeared in the *Washington Post*. Twenty-five and a half months later,

Richard Nixon's presidency had unraveled and he resigned in disgrace.

The desire to be able to affect the course of events—to have power—is one motivation of young idealists who go into the news business. At the moment of Nixon's resignation, that motive seemed vindicated. Soon, however, the news media became intoxicated with new-found power. The rest of us, as onlookers, became infatuated with the media. As we found cracks in the structures of our institutions and feet of clay on our leaders, we eagerly snapped up articles, books, television dramas and films that glorified newspeople as idealistic, determined investigators who dug until they found the facts to humble the proud, the mighty and the wrongdoers.

All the President's Men, the film version of Woodward and Bernstein's popular memoir about uncovering the Watergate scandal, was a case in point. Gary Arnold, reviewing it in the *Washington Post*,[2] described the film, starring Robert Redford and Dustin Hoffman, as a "full-scale salute to the *Post* during its finest hour."

The Media High continued. Newspapers ran front-page stories on the business of gathering news. Television network bidding wars over anchormen became major news stories in themselves. One television series, "Lou Grant," depicted the editor of a daily newspaper and his reporters as indefatigable pursuers of truth and justice, while business people in the series were invariably shown as greedy and conniving.

Modern-day advocacy journalism, a product of the sixties, cast the reporter as not just a chronicler but an activist for causes. This form of journalism remained alive and well during the years of the Media High. Its thesis seemed vindicated in the seventies, when seemingly the only person you could trust—the only one whose integrity was intact—was the crusading reporter.

Warren Hinckle, former editor of *Ramparts* and a long-time practitioner of advocacy journalism for leftist causes, said this about his work in 1981: "What journalism is all about is to attack everybody. First you decide what's wrong, then you go out to find the facts to support that view, and then you generate enough controversy to attract attention."[3]

The *Aim Report*, published by the conservative watchdog organization Accuracy in Media (AIM), frequently cites a quotation of Karen DeYoung, the foreign news editor of the *Washington Post*. While teaching a journalism class at the left-leaning Institute for Policy Studies in Washington, DeYoung, discussing Central America, was quoted as saying, "Most journalists now, most Western journalists at least, are very eager to seek out guerrilla groups, leftist groups, because you assume they must be the good guys."[4]

During the seventies, newsrooms across the United States developed a new crop of "investigative" reporters in the Woodward-Bernstein mold. One day in 1975, traveling with my then client, Ronald Reagan, to a political speaking engagement in Denver, I met a young reporter with one of the newspapers there who had been sent to cover the Reagan speech. "Do you usually cover politics?" I asked. "No, I'm an *investigative* reporter," he replied. What did that entail, I asked. "Oh, I poke around city hall," he said. It turned out that he mostly covered city council meetings.

Jim Lehrer of the PBS's "McNeill-Lehrer News Hour," reflected on the intoxicating effects of media power at a University of Texas press symposium in 1981. About journalists he said, "I think our major problem...is that somehow we have gotten it into our heads that we are truly the special people of this world because we happen to be in journalism."[5] He went on to relate that he first became interested in sports writing in school "because I was too small to play sports."

Such criticism of newspeople by one of their own is not common. More often, media people see themselves as surrogates for the public. ABC's David Brinkley probably summed up the view of many of his professional peers when he said on the network's "Nightline" program in early December 1983, "If we are not surrogates [for the public] we are nothing." Addressing his remarks to Mobil Corporation vice president of public affairs Herbert Schmertz, Brinkley went on to make the point that if journalists were "nothing," neither Schmertz nor anyone else would know what was going on anywhere. Brinkley had defined "surrogate" as "one who acts in another's behalf."

Noting this, the *Washington Times* peppery columnist John Lofton wrote, "Mr. Brinkley, say what you want about the press. But *please* don't say you guys are acting on my behalf. I don't need you as a surrogate. Why? Because I think that 'primarily—predominantly, the press, at least in this part of the country, is somewhat liberal...I think that very often...a person of notably conservative views has to go a little further...to get a fair shake than a liberal does.'" At that point, Lofton reminded Brinkley that the words in quotes were his own, from an interview with the *New Yorker's* Elizabeth Drew on July 13, 1971.[6]

The media-as-surrogate idea is closely related to the notion of "the people's right to know," which is frequently cited by newspeople to legitimize their demand to have access to any information they seek. Yet, search as you may, you will find no references in the Constitution of the United States to "the people's right to know."

THE MEDIA AND GRENADA

The right-to-know argument was cited by many in the news media following the U.S. landings in Grenada in October 1983. Angry that they had been barred from accompanying the task force to Grenada, several of the nation's most influential media gave the military action negative treatment. They were almost universally critical of the Department of Defense's decision to keep them out for the first 48 hours. The reason was obvious and probably accounted for the defensive tone of the media: the DOD did not trust them to keep a secret.

If the media expected their critical drumbeat to be taken up by the public, they were wrong. Political analyst William Schneider, writing in the *National Journal*, noted that the media treated the Reagan administration's decision to exclude the press from the landings as if it were an unconstitutional act and "deprived" the people of their "right to know." He wrote, "Judging from the evidence, the public did not feel particularly deprived. The polls show considerable approval of the decision to keep the press out. Indeed, resentment of the press seemed to explode in the aftermath of Grenada."[7]

An example showed up in a *Los Angeles Times* nationwide poll conducted in November 1983. By a margin of 9 percent (52 to 41), respondents told the pollsters that they approved of the denial of "unrestricted press coverage" of the Grenada action.

NBC reported that among 500 letters and telephone calls about Grenada, viewers supported the press ban by five to one.[8] *Editor and Publisher*, a trade magazine for the newspaper business, surveyed a dozen U.S. dailies and found that letters to the editor ran three to one in favor of the administration's press action.[9]

Secretary of State George Shultz may have summed up the public mood when he told executives of the Gannett Co., Inc. that in World War II "reporters were involved all along. And, on the whole, they were on our side." Now, he added, "it seems as though reporters are always against us....They're always seeking to report something that's going to screw things up."[10]

President Reagan's October 27 television address solidified public support for the Grenada action. The day before the speech, a *Washington Post*-ABC News poll showed support for the administration's actions was 52 percent to 37 percent. The day after the speech, the figures went to 65 to 27.

All this is a far cry from the days of the Media High in the seventies. Indeed, the public's negative mood about media complaints of the Grenada action spelled the end of the nation's Media High altogether.

SIGNS OF THE MEDIA IN TROUBLE

There had been a number of earlier signs that we were coming off the Media High, for example:

◆ The 1981 film *Absence of Malice*, which depicted a reckless reporter ruining lives in pursuit of a story

◆ The cooked-up story of "Jimmy," an eight-year-old heroin addict, by *Washington Post* reporter Janet Cooke

◆ A rash of other journalistic fakeries uncovered in the wake of the Cooke episode

◆ The libel suit by Carl Galloway, a Los Angeles physician, against CBS' "60 Minutes." Although it led to an acquittal, the trial nevertheless embarrassed Dan Rather and exposed some of "60 Minutes'" more slapdash techniques at entrapping interview subjects.

The poineer in "ambush" interviews and a model for imitators over the years, "60 Minutes" itself provided a fitting postscript to the Media High on New Year's Day 1984, when it used one segment of the program to cover television coaches who work for corporate clients to prepare them for interviews on the likes of "60 Minutes."

Glamorizing the professionals who help interviewees joust with "60 Minutes'" interviewers was recognition by this popular show that people weren't just answering questions any more, they were actually talking back to the media.

Further evidence that "60 Minutes" sensed a newly critical mood in the public was its inclusion—after the Galloway case—of at least one upbeat "human interest" feature on every Sunday program.

Similarly, the *Washington Post* seemed to lose some of its bite after the Janet Cooke incident. The exposure of the story of "Jimmy" as a fake was a serious blow to the credibility of the *Post* and, by implication, all news media.

Janet Cooke and "Jimmy"

What caused all this? Cooke's story, appearing in the *Post* on September 28, 1980, told of the life and times of an eight-year-old boy in a Washington, D.C. neighborhood. His name, according to the reporter, was Jimmy and and he had become a heroin addict after first being given a sniff of the drug by his mother's boyfriend.

Before her article was published, Cooke told her editors that she had promised Jimmy and his mother anonymity in exchange for being able to tell their story. She also told the editors that the mother's boyfriend had threatened her life if she disclosed their whereabouts.

Publication of "Jimmy's World" brought a quick, sharp response from city authorities. The mayor and police chief sent a task force of social workers and police to locate "Jimmy," in order to get him medical treatment. When he could not be located, Mayor Marion Barry publicly expressed doubt that Jimmy existed.

It was not until more than six months later, however, that Janet Cooke's story began to unravel. In April 1981, the *Post* learned that Pulitzer officials had discovered that her autobiographical submission for the prize contained untruths. They learned, for example, that Cooke had not been graduated *magna cum laude* from Vassar but had actually attended that college for only one year. Similarly, the Associated Press told *Post* officials that it had learned from Ohio sources that Cooke had not received a master's degree from the University of Toledo, as she had claimed.

One by one, in interviews with *Post* officials, Cooke confessed to the inaccuracies in her resume. It was then that the officials insisted she prove Jimmy's existence. The city editor drove her to the neighborhood where she said Jimmy lived, but she could not locate his house. Meanwhile, *Post* editors went over the notes and tapes she had used in preparing the story. They could find no references to meetings with Jimmy and his family. It began to dawn on them that Jimmy was an invention, a composite of the lives Cooke had heard about from social workers and other specialists.

At a final meeting, Cooke confessed the fabrication and resigned from the *Post*. Why had she risked her career on such a fabrication? Job pressure and competition seemed to be at the heart of the problem. She had originally spent two months looking for a "Jimmy," and when she could not find one, she worried about how it would appear to her colleagues. "If I could not produce a story, then how was I to justify my time?...My whole mind-set was pretty much in the *Washington Post* mentality, which was that he ['Jimmy'] must be there and it's being covered up," she said.[11]

This "mind-set," as many business executives facing sharp questioning by skeptical reporters have discovered, is not restricted to the *Washington Post*.

Within a month of the revelation of the "Jimmy's World" fabrication (April 1981), a *New York Daily News* columnist, Michael Daly, admitted that he had invented a British soldier who, according to his report, shot a Northern Ireland teenager in cold blood. At the same time, Daly admitted altering factual details in other columns but contended that this did not impair his vision of the truth.

Even the *New York Times* was not immune. A few months after the Cooke and Daly revelations, it turned out that a *Times Sunday Magazine* story by free-lance writer Christopher Jones, purporting to be an eyewitness account of conditions in Cambodia, had actually been concocted in the comfort of his home in Spain. To make matters worse, parts of the story had been lifted from a 1930 novel by André Malraux.

All three newspapers acted quickly to get to the bottom of these fakeries, but all three incidents underscored the vulnerability of editors to overly ambitious reporters. In the *Washington Post's* story about the withdrawal of Janet Cooke's Pulitzer prize, its executive editor, Benjamin C. Bradlee, said that a newspaper's credibility, its greatest asset, is heavily dependent on that paper's reporters. "When that integrity is questioned and found wanting, the wounds are grievous and there is nothing to do but come clean with our readers."[12]

Absence of Malice

Getting the story is what *Absence of Malice* is all about, too. The film is the antithesis of *All the President's Men*, in which the newspeople could do no wrong. In *Absence of Malice*, the investigative reporter of a Miami newspaper is suckered into using a false file planted by an unscrupulous U. S. attorney to frame the son of a racketeer for involvement in the disappearance of a labor leader. The reporter "goes" with several accusatory stories without proper verification and her prying leads an unstable woman to kill herself.

Several critics from the media took the film to task, claiming that it did not accurately depict the way newspeople behave. They cited the film reporter's failure to interview the suspect before writing the story as evidence of their claim that she is not like "real" reporters. That may be, but the significant thing about *Absence of Malice* is that it paints an unflattering portrait of a profession that only a few years before was being lionized. And it shows us a breed of reporter many business people have encountered: bright, skeptical of protestations of innocence and single-minded about "getting the story."

Absence of Malice was written by no antimedia paranoid. The author, Kurt Leudtke, left a 20-year career as a reporter and editor to become a screenwriter.

Leudtke, whose career has included stints with the *Miami Herald* and the *Detroit Free Press*, told *New York Times* reporter Jonathan Friendly that he was being attacked by newspeople who "have just been infuriated and said, 'You're playing into the hands of the current mood of the country. The public is going to rise up and strike us down, and you've done a very damaging thing.'"[13]

Leudtke maintained that the press was too strong an institution to collapse under the weight of criticism. And, despite defensiveness about the film on the part of media people, one of their groups—the Reporters' Committee for Freedom of the Press—was the beneficiary of the film's premiere in Washington, D.C. Friendly, in his *Times* article, noted ironically that the back of the invitations to the premiere stated, "This film ought to serve as a dramatic object lesson of the difficult and heavy obligation professional journalists have to be accurate and thorough while pursuing the free press values of the First Amendment."

Galloway vs. "60 Minutes"

If *Absence of Malice* served as an object lesson, the libel suit brought by Los Angeles physician Carl Galloway against CBS upped the ante. CBS' "60 Minutes" had accused Dr. Galloway of involvement in a scheme to defraud health insurance companies. Galloway insisted he had nothing to do with it and sued. On the witness stand, CBS' Dan Rather said he had put in several telephone calls to Galloway but that they were not returned. He related that in his experience failure to return his telephone calls tended to confirm his suspicions about the subject of his investigation. In other words, Galloway was presumed to be "guilty."

What Galloway had to prove, in order to sustain the libel charge, was that CBS intended to defame him; that it acted out of malice. That is a tough case to prove. In a 1977 opinion, a U.S. District Court judge defined "malice" thus: "In the context of a libel suit 'actual malice' simply does not mean ill will or spite. Rather, 'malice' must be taken to mean fraudulent, knowing publication of a falsehood, or reckless disregard of falsity. And we note that reckless does not mean grossly negligent, its common use, but rather, intentional disregard."[14]

Galloway's lawyers did not satisfy the definition of "actual malice" in their pleadings, and "60 Minutes," which has been involved in more than 150 libel suits, was acquitted. Yet, while Galloway won no damages from CBS, Rather's testimony, widely reported, tended to reinforce the growing public perception of the media as being self-interested, careless and irresponsible. Film taken by the "60 Minutes" camera crew, not used on the air but shown at the trial, further debunked the reporter-as-crusader myth. In the footage, interviews were rehearsed or rehashed, in order to lead interviewees to the "right" answers.

Statistics suggest that libel suits are an increasingly successful—if extreme—way of talking back to the media. According to Stanford University law professor Marc Franklin, who monitors and analyzes libel cases, 85 percent of 106 major libel verdicts by juries since 1975 have resulted in defeats for the media defendants. This prompted *St. Petersburg Times* editor Eugene Patterson to remark, "Juries are the American people. They want to punish us."[15]

Are all the libel verdicts evidence of a pattern or are they coincidental? The question is virtually impossible to answer; however, defensiveness on the part of media people suggests they think Patterson is correct. Each new libel suit brings much hand-wringing in the media about "the chilling effect" a verdict in favor of the plaintiff will have on free inquiry. While there is no evidence that any such libel verdict has resulted in anything other than greater care being taken in checking stories, the media reaction is always the same.

There is little doubt that many people in the news media confuse their acknowledged roles as observers, reporters, analysts and commentators with that of self-appointed protectors of all aspects of American democracy. It is when this confusion of roles clashes with public perceptions of what journalists are or should be that tension results.

NBC's John Chancellor, in a commentary (and so labeled) on "The Nightly News," just after the Grenada military action, said, "The American government is doing whatever it wants to, without any representative of the American people watching what it is doing." All this was said with a straight face, as if the government were not led by elected officials and as if all those soldiers and marines were not themselves members of the American body politic.

Chancellor was speaking earnestly, and what he had in mind was that the media were the missing "representative of the American people." It was another way of stating the old surrogate-for-the-people argument. As we have seen, however, the public emphatically rejected the media for this role in Grenada, and there is no evidence at hand to suggest that the public accords this role to the media in other situations today, either.

This was not always the case. By the mid-seventies, the news media had become what pollster John Bartolomeo calls "a sovereign institution," inspiring more public confidence than such institutions of our society as business/industry and labor unions. In 1976, according to a survey by the National Opinion Research Center, 29 percent of the people had "a great deal of confidence in the press." That, as it turned out, was the high point of "sovereignty" for the media.

What did this sovereignty mean while it lasted? It meant we suspended our questioning of the motives of reporters, for one thing. It meant we assumed that those in the media had higher, purer motives than those engaged in the work of government and business. After all, hadn't the media shown us, after Watergate and Vietnam, that we had to be suspicious about the motives of the mighty?

The cynicism and suspiciousness that marked the reaction of journalists to events of the 1970s seemed to sour into a pervasive negativism and have, by the mid-eighties, brought our Media High and the sovereignty of the media to an end.

By 1983, the National Opinion Research Center registered only 13.7 percent of the public as having "a great deal of confidence in the press." This was near the cellar in confidence ratings, down there with television (12.7%) and Congress (10.2%)—and a far cry from the leader, medicine (52.3%), or even banks (24.1%). It represents a loss of public confidence by almost half in just seven years.

Our Media High may be over, but media negativism has not gone away. That is bad news for executives who have to face the media. Why all this negativism among journalists? What are they after? What should you watch for in dealing with them? That is what Chapter Two is all about.

2/ Accentuate the Negative?

During World War II there was a popular song with the title "Accentuate the Positive." The lyrics began with the title, then went on with, "Ee-lim-in-ate the negative, and don't mess with Mr. In-between."

While millions of Americans probably have optimistic dispositions that allow them to "accentuate the positive" a good deal of the time, it is a tougher thing to do for those in the news business. News, by its very nature, is that which is out of the ordinary. Disasters large and small, economic changes and uncertainties, wrongdoing in high places, violence—all are the stuff of which news is made. We are ever curious about the world around us, and the news media satisfy our curiosity by blanketing the globe with reports 24 hours a day.

Until the mid-sixties, when new journalism and advocacy journalism[16] burst upon the scene, reporters served largely as chroniclers of events. The "objective" style of reporting prevailed (indeed, still does), with the reporter being expected to present the facts (who, what, when, where, why, how), remain neutral and not pass judgment.

New journalism abandoned the old pyramid style of reporting (which started with the five "w's" and an "h," then elaborated on each), in favor of colorful narration intended to convey a sense of immediacy and intimacy lacking in the objective style.

New journalism spawned the use of composites, descriptions of seemingly real people and events that were actually fragments of experience and impressions in the writer's mind, stitched together and given specific identities in order to bring more order to what the writer was observing.

Whether this technique serves journalism-let alone the public—is a matter of continuing controversy. The Janet Cooke composite character "Jimmy," the nonexistent eight-year-old heroin addict, cost Cooke her Pulitzer prize and her job. It also cost the *Washington Post* an immeasurable loss of credibility.

More recently, the *New Yorker* became embroiled in a controversy over the use of composites. It began with a June 18, 1984 interview in the *Wall Street Journal* by Joanne Lipman, in which *New Yorker* writer Alastair Reid admitted to having used fiction in his ostensibly factual *New Yorker* articles on a number of occasions. For example, he cited a 1961 article, "Letter from Barcelona," in which he described a colorful small bar that had been a favorite of his. He described the bar patrons watching a televised speech by Generalissimo Francisco Franco, hooting at it and arguing about politics. In fact, Reid told his interviewer, the bar was closed at the time, and he had watched the Franco speech on a friend's television set. The colorful scene he had described was a composite of many conversations and impressions he had had over a period of time.

"In reporting, at times, we have to go much further than the strictly factual. Facts are part of the perceived whole," the *New York Times* quoted Reid as saying in its issue of June 19, 1984.

In the *Journal* interview, Reid related other occasions when he fictionalized facts for the benefit of "the perceived whole." In one case, in the *New Yorker's* (June 1982) "Talk of the Town" section, he wrote observations attributed to "a flinty old friend…from the country" who had reluctantly attended his grandniece's graduation from Yale. The "flinty old friend" was Reid himself, and the "grandniece" was his own son.

Do these stretchings of the truth make any difference? William Shawn, editor of the *New Yorker*, rushed to the defense of his writer. The *New York Times'* June 19th story reported Shawn as saying, "It doesn't mean one should discard facts or shouldn't respect facts, but the truth has to include something that goes beyond facts."

Goes beyond facts? How far, and who is to judge? Shawn's fuzzy idea of the role that facts play in journalism served to back up Reid's own casual view of his writing methods. He was said to have "not a single twinge of guilt." To this he added a dash of self-pity: "I just feel carved up."[17]

A number of Reid's peers had a different view. Fred Friendly, former president of CBS News and emeritus professor at the Columbia University Graduate School of Journalism, was quoted as saying, "A composite is a euphemism for a lie. It's disorderly, it's dishonest and it's not journalism."[18]

Reid's fellow *New Yorker* writer Ken Auletta said that Reid was wrong, and he made the point that readers should be informed if a writer is going to take shortcuts—that is, fictionalize a story.

The Reid incident was an embarrassment to the *New Yorker*, which has a reputation for meticulous checking of facts in its articles and stories. Indeed, it has eight full-time fact checkers. Like all other media, however, it must rely ultimately on the honesty of its writers.

If new journalism involves stretching the truth in the service of some vision of the craft as a higher art form, advocacy journalism goes a step further. Growing out of the student rebellions of the sixties and disillusionment over Vietnam and Watergate, advocacy journalism took the position that objectivity and neutrality on the issues of the day were impossible and undesirable. Instead—the argument went—the writer should week to convince others of the rightness of his or her cause and point of view. This was a sharp departure from the objective style that had dominated U.S. news media for most of the 20th century.

Enrollment in college journalism schools increased, roughly in inverse proportion to the decline of public confidence in the institutions of American society. Young people—looking for heroes and for outlets for their own idealism—thought they saw those heroes in the crusading reporters and commentators practicing advocacy journalism. They flocked to follow them.

New journalism and advocacy journalism did not converge. One was largely concerned with style, the other tendentious. Tom Wolfe, a leader in the new journalism movement and a successful author of many books (and generally considered as something of a conservative), never really practiced advocacy journalism, in which a political agenda is the writer's paramount pursuit.

Advocacy journalism has not disappeared. Geraldo Rivera, ABC television investigative reporter, admitted afterward that his reportage of the Panama Canal treaty issue in 1977 and 1978 was affected by his strong belief that the treaties had to be ratified.

The *Washington Post* has given us a more recent example, beginning a front-page news article on the Grenada military action with this sarcasm: "President Reagan yesterday celebrated the 'heroic rescue' of American medical students from Grenada in a ceremony climaxing a White House effort to put the best political face on the invasion of the Caribbean island and the terrorist bombing in Lebanon that killed at least 230 servicemen."[19]

WHY THEY BECAME REPORTERS

Accentuating the negative? Yes, but why? Most of today's generation of journalists formed their view of the world during a time when they found that traditional leaders had feet of clay, or so it seemed. Many of these leaders were seen as adversaries in the eyes of the young idealists. Watergate, in particular, with its hero-journalists Woodward and Bernstein, spawned dreams among innumerable young journalists of finding a potential "Watergate" in every story they were assigned. To crack a big story about wrongdoing can mean fame, money and peer respect. It is a form of power, and a desire for power—to improve the world—is a fundamental motivation of many people who go into journalism. Yet because news by its nature is largely negative, the power these journalists wield is largely negative. They can tear down, but there is little they can build up.

In *Reporting*, perhaps the definitive book about the business, Lou Cannon, the *Washington Post's* White House correspondent verifies that many people become reporters "because they seek to have some social impact on the world."[20]

In interviewing many professional peers for his book, Cannon found that a plurality had been steered toward journalism as a result of some parental influence.

He claims that "reporting also satisfied a need in some people of explaining things to their fellow human beings," and that many people who are attracted to careers in journalism come from small towns. He adds, "Journalism in America always has been a pathway to the top for talented people who lacked money or the right connections."[21]

Cannon thinks the news business may be a magnet to shy people, too. In *Reporting*, he quotes columnist and former *New York Times* correspondent Richard Reeves as saying, "I could go to a party and never say a word to anyone—I don't know how to begin a conversation. But if I say, 'Excuse me, I'm Dick Reeves of the *Times*,' that breaks the ice for me and I can deal with the situation."[22]

Cannon believes that first newspapers and later television have served as magnets for "the shy, curious small-town kid" who wants to make a mark on the world.

Over the years I have had some personal confirmation of Cannon's "small-town kid" theory. As a member of Ronald

Reagan's senior staff in the 1976 and 1980 presidential campaigns, I had many occasions to socialize after hours with members of the press corps traveling with us. Relaxed, most were unaffected and affable. A large number hailed from small towns, especially from the Midwest.

Although, as Cannon points out, the motivations behind the career choice of journalism are diverse, the desire for fame and—for some—fortune should come as no surprise. Ambition exists to a degree in all of us and it affects the way we make decisions both large and small. To paraphrase F. Scott Fitzgerald, however, reporters are different from you and me. Their ambition operates against the backdrop of an imperative: Get the story and get it first!

This imperative is a constant in U.S. journalism and it may lead the reporter to skirt the edges of the law, engage in ethically dubious behavior or be just plain obnoxious. (Residential "stakeouts" provide frequent examples of this last point.)

Today, most Americans get their headlines from television. Newspapers are in transition from their old role of being the first to bring you the news, to their new one of being interpreters of the significance of the news. For the time being, they are behaving as if they were still breaking the news. Thus, newspaper reporters, just as much as television and radio reporters, are still driven by the get-the-story-and-get-it-first imperative.

If a reporter is assigned to "get" a particular story and you are part of that story, you will quickly learn that the reporter's ambition, put through the filter of his or her experience, can have an effect on the way you shape your responses. If you allow yourself to be intimidated by the sense of urgency in this encounter you may say things you will regret later.

Reporters will nearly always tell you they are "on deadline." Indeed, they may have little or no time to verify assertions or countercharges. They may have had no time to check what their own news organization has previously reported on the subject. And chances are they will have had no time to do research on your industry or profession.

The reporter will make a near-instantaneous determination about your "credibility" in the course of a brief interview, probably on the telephone. You need to be prepared, for you will be dealing not only with the reporter's ingrained skepticism, but also with his or her ambition to get a story that will contribute to personal career advancement.

The production deadlines of news media put a premium on speed in gathering material for a story. When speed competes with the need for accuracy, speed often wins out. Thus, the business executive who is being interviewed may make what he or she thinks is clear distinction between two facts, only to find them fused—and confused—in the story that appears.

In *Reporting*, Lou Cannon says that "the reporter's view that he is performing a sacred calling can cloak him with an annoying self-righteousness about his mission which ordinary Americans find disturbing. Out of this attitude of mission sometimes arises an insensitivity and a mistaken belief that a reporter is entitled to ask anyone anything at any time."[23]

A reporter's reform-minded idealism, buffeted by encounters with corruption, graft and scandal in government or business, may turn permanently sour. It may turn into the persistent negativism many people automatically associate with the news media today.

David Gergen, chief of communications at the White House during the first three years of Ronald Reagan's presidency, described what he saw as the self-defeating effects of this negativism in an interview as he left government:

> The press is beginning to suffer from the same kind of criticism and loss of confidence that other major institutions have experienced. The American people tend to distrust large and powerful organizations that are seen as trying to serve their own ends. Not only has the press become a huge institution within our society, but too many who now work as journalists are seen as serving not the public but their own private interests—trying to make a buck, attract an audience, grind an axe and the like.[24]

THE MEDIA ELITE

One of the problems that seems to be feeding the public's impatience with news media negativism is the fact that, politically and philosophically, the elite of the media world are, indeed, not like most of the rest of us.

In recent years, a large number of Americans, ranging from a plurality to a strong majority, have described themselves in polls as "conservative." For example, political analyst Alan Baron says, "Asked to define themselves on a scale of 1 (most liberal) to 7 (most conservative) through 1980, voters consistently gave themselves a 4."[25]

In contrast, the media elite, surveyed by S. Robert Lichter and Stanley Rothman in a landmark study conducted in 1979 and 1980 (and published in 1981),[26] said they had voted for George McGovern (81%) over Richard Nixon (19%) in 1972 and, in the four presidential elections between 1964 and 1976, gave no Republican candidate more than 19 percent of their vote.

Lichter and Rothman conducted hour-long interviews of 240 print and broadcast journalists on such major media as the *New York Times*, *Wall Street Journal*, *Washington Post*, *Newsweek*, *Time*, *U.S. News & World Report*, and in the news departments of ABC, CBS, NBC and PBS.

The authors set out to learn about the backgrounds of these members of the media elite and to determine their attitudes toward American society and their own profession. The researchers selected their interview subjects at random from among those executives responsible for news content. From their survey, the researchers drew this statistical profile of the media elite:

White (95%); male (79%); college graduate (93%); postgraduate study (55%); annual income over $30,000 (78%); income over $50,000 (46%); liberal (54%); religion "none" (50%).

Compared with the 54 percent who described themselves as left-of-center, only 19 percent put themselves to the right of center.

The outlook of the media elite is secular. Only 50 percent subscribe to any religion and only 8 percent said they are regular churchgoers. Eighty-six percent said they seldom or never attend religious services.

On social issues they are liberal or libertarian. Ninety percent agreed that a woman has a right to decide for herself whether to have an abortion (79 percent said they "agree strongly"). Fifty-four percent said they did not regard adultery as wrong. Only 15 percent agreed "strongly" with the assertion that extramarital affairs were wrong.

On economic matters, the media elite have ambivalent feelings. While only 13 percent agreed with the proposition that big business should be taken over by the government, 68 percent agreed with the idea that "government should reduce the income gap." Forty-eight percent agreed that "government should guarantee jobs." These media leaders are not for equality of results, however, for 86 percent agreed that "people with more ability should earn more." This is not surprising, considering that a large majority of the media elite earn more than the U.S. median income for a family of four.[27]

Although 70 percent agreed that private enterprise is fair to working people, and 63 percent favored less government regulation of business, the opposite side of that coin was the belief of 49 percent of those interviewed that "the very structure of our society causes people to feel alienated."

The commitment of the media elite to free enterprise capitalism seems to be rooted in their own prosperity, but it is diluted by a thread of guilt about world problems that runs through their answers. For example, 56 percent agreed that "American exploitation has contributed to Third World poverty." This charge, frequently made by some Third World countries, is not the only one echoed by the journalistic leaders. Fifty-seven percent also said that America's usage of the world's natural resources is "immoral." Only 25 percent agreed with the statement that "Western assistance has helped the Third World."

The concluding section of the Lichter-Rothman study addressed itself to the question of who should direct society toward its goals. Since many of the media elite identified their values with those of social liberalism, the scholars wanted to know how they evaluated those who competed with them. They asked the media people to rate seven leadership groups in the United States in two ways: first, according to the amount of influence each group wields in relation to the others; second, according to the way the media elite feel each group *should* wield influence.

Following is the media elite's *perception* of the influence of various groups, in descending order:

Business
Media
Unions
Consumer groups
Intellectuals
Black leaders
Feminists

The media elite assigned relatively less influence to the unions than to business and themselves; however, the other four groups were clustered tightly together, far behind the unions.

Following is the order in which the media would *prefer* these groups to have influence in American society:

Media
Consumer groups
Intellectuals
Blacks
Business
Feminists
Unions

Thus emerges the underlying hostility of the media elite toward business. James Flanigan, writing of the Lichter-

Rothman study in the *Los Angeles Times*, has another view: "...'envy' would be as good a word as 'hostility' for what the research found."[28]

Lichter and Rothman also asked 216 middle and upper level business executives at seven *Fortune 500* companies to make the same perception/preference ratings as the media elite had done. Not surprisingly, the views of the business leaders were opposite to those of the media elite. They saw the media as clearly the most powerful institution in American society. Unions were a distant second and business third, followed by the other groups. Business, like the media elite, told the researchers that their group should be at the top of the influence ladder.

Flanigan of the *Los Angeles Times* asks, "What should the media and business do? They should get on with the jobs society gives them—the one to build the economy, the other to explain it clearly. And stop giving themselves airs about their influence over the American people." That is good advice in the abstract, but hard to follow if media reports imply that your company's profits are unjustified.

TOMORROW'S JOURNALISTS

Lichter and Rothman, joined by Linda Lichter, a research associate at Columbia University, followed their 1979-80 study of the media elite with one of students at Columbia's School of Journalism—tomorrow's media elite—published in 1982.

If business could take little comfort from the earlier study, it will get almost none from the later one. "Our findings show that these aspiring journalists are more liberal in attitude, more cosmopolitan in background and more out of step with prevailing American beliefs than those already at the top of the profession," the authors say.[29]

The researchers interviewed, at random, 28 candidates for master's degrees in journalism at Columbia. The questions assayed their backgrounds and their views on political movements, leaders and the trustworthiness of the media. A number of the questions were similar to those asked of the media elite in the earlier survey.

Contrary to Lou Cannon's conclusion in *Reporting* that many journalists come from small towns and see the profession as a way upward, the Lichter and Rothman "...found very few Horatio Algers among...aspiring journalists, 70 percent of whom have college-educated fathers"[30] (compared with 40 percent of the working journalists in the earlier survey).

In both the media elite and journalism student group, they found that only 20 percent came from blue-collar family backgrounds. Fifty-seven percent of the students described their family income as above average (45 percent of the working journalists did so).

While 54 percent of the working journalists in the first study described themselves as politically liberal, the figure jumped to 85 percent in the student survey. The percentage describing themselves as conservative dropped from 19 to 11. This held true in the students' voting patterns. In the 1980 presidential election, while 52 percent of all voters were choosing Ronald Reagan, only four percent of the journalism students did so. Fifty-nine percent of them voted for Jimmy Carter; 29 percent for John Anderson.

If the attitudes of today's journalists toward business worry you, things will get bleaker in the future. That is the message from the Columbia journalism students. While the working journalists in the first survey wanted business to have less power than they thought it had, 70 percent said they thought the private enterprise system is fair to workers. Only one-quarter of the students shared this view; nearly 40 percent of them favored government ownership of corporations.

Seventy-five percent of the students believe the United States exploits Third World countries (compared with 56 percent of the media elite), and 89 percent believe that the main goal of U.S. foreign policy is to protect American business (compared with 80 percent of the working journalists).

The students' attitude toward society's leaders can be summed up in a word: negative. They were asked to rate American and world leaders on a scale ranging from "strong approval" to "strong disapproval." Toward the bottom was Ronald Reagan; toward the top, Ralph Nader and Gloria Steinem.

The students were also asked to rate various media on reliability. They said the *New York Times, Washington Post* and the leftist *New York Review of Books* were "highly reliable." They also gave high marks to left-of-center opinion journals such as *The Nation* and *The New Republic*. Two conservative magazines, *National Review* and *Commentary*, were at the bottom of their list.

In two respects, the composition of the student group was markedly different from that of the working media elite: It was 45 percent female (versus 21 percent in the earlier group) and it included 21 percent from racial minorities, compared with only 5 percent in the first survey group.

Despite racial and gender composition more reflective of the population than the earlier group, the student survey group gives business executives no cause for comfort. The authors conclude, "Although we cannot predict how their views may change as they mature and become professionals, it is clear that they will come to journalism with firmly established liberal attitudes and views that place them at considerable odds with Middle American values."[31]

HERD INSTINCT

Journalists may think of themselves as strong individualists. Indeed, the writing style of some, such as Tom Wolfe, is highly individualistic. Still, reporters assigned to a particular story are under pressure to stay ahead of the competition, and they harbor a desire not to be caught on the end of a journalistic limb. They do not like to be very far from the mainstream interpretation of a particular story or event.

Former U.S. senator and presidential candidate Eugene

McCarthy characterized the journalistic herd instinct this way: "Journalists are like blackbirds on a telephone wire. One flies away and they all fly away. One comes back and they all come back."[32]

An example of the herd instinct at work was the sudden flood of coverage of U.S. Sen. Gary Hart after he upset former Vice President Walter Mondale in the New Hampshire Democratic primary in February 1984. Prior to New Hampshire (and the Iowa caucuses a few days before), Hart rated only occasional coverage because he commanded a less than 5 percent support in the polls. What few stories did appear concentrated on his apparent inability to get his Kennedyesque campaign off the ground. Following the New Hampshire upset, Mondale's coverage suddenly focused on a candidacy in sharp decline. At the same time, Hart's "new ideas" campaign got extensive coverage, almost breathless in tone. Conservative columnist Patrick Buchanan noted in a *Washington Times* column on March 7 that, "caught totally off guard by Mr. Hart's victory[,]...the media are now overcompensating at Mr. Mondale's expense."

In the business world, the 1979 Three Mile Island nuclear power plant accident in Pennsylvania generated almost universal negative media coverage, largely as a result of the confusion of information in the early stages of the developing story. The problem was compounded by the unwillingness of utility spokesmen to appear to be forthcoming in their dealings with the media.

The media herd instinct worked more positively in the 1982 Tylenol tampering case in Chicago. After initial confusion, and political overraction by then Chicago Mayor Jane Byrne, the story began to turn around as a result of the candid handling of the matter by Johnson & Johnson, parent company of the Tylenol manufacturer. James Burke, the Johnson & Johnson chairman, and other senior executives were fully accessible to the media and the company made no secret of the market drubbing it had taken as a result of the tampering (still unsolved at this writing). Johnson & Johnson recalled the packages of Tylenol that were vulnerable to tampering and later relaunched the product in new tamper-proof packages. Within 15 months Tylenol had regained nearly all of its lost share of the market. While advertising played an important role, the fact that the news media responded sympathetically to Johnson & Johnson's candor certainly helped.

You may not think that the dozens of political reporters based in Washington are relevant to your organization. But if your organization is ever involved in supporting or opposing major legislation, or in Congressional hearings or oversight investigations, it may well come to the attention of some of these reporters. When the issue is a political one, reporters tend to watch for the reactions of certain "bell cow" journalists. The *Washington Post's* highly regarded David Broder, the *New York Times'* Hedrick Smith and the *Wall Street Journal's* Al Hunt are in this category. For media outside the New York-Washington axis, the *Times*, the *Post* and the *Journal* are bell-cow media in almost any major category of story. (The first two have their own news services to which many other newspapers subscribe.)

The herd instinct works overseas, too. European journalists, for example, tend to shape their view of the United States from reading the *Times* and the *Post*. Journalist-historian George Urban made this point in a discussion in 1983 with then U.S. Ambassador to the United Nations Jeane Kirkpatrick. He said that the widespread belief of European journalists that the *New York Times* and the *Washington Post* are "authentic voices of American public opinion" can be "highly misleading."

Kirkpatrick responded, "Sometimes more than misleading. On a good many issues, these two papers express the opposite of what the U.S. public feels and stands for. Often their views represent only the thinking of an influential but narrow band of the East Coast cultural elite."[33]

The herd instinct can be hurtful if you are the subject of a negative story, not only because one medium may set the tone of the story, but also because of the tendency of many reporters to pick up material for their stories from previously published or broadcast stories that may include blind sources. This can be especially true of weekend wire service stories. Verification is hard to obtain on weekends, when most newspapers and television stations are staffed very lightly. The tendency to trust the assertions of sources in wire service stories is therefore great. I have been involved in wire service stories breaking on weekends, in which assumptions were made without proper verification. As a result, misleading conclusions about the subjects were repeated endlessly across the country by member newspapers that tore the wire copy off the machine and printed it verbatim.

Another disturbing aspect of the journalistic herd instinct is the tendency of reporters, in the interest of time and space, to oversimplify descriptions of people, places and events. According to David Broder, "More sins are committed by journalists through their habit of labeling and categorizing people and situations than by any other means. Seeking to impose a simple-minded order on the confusing and ambiguous events and characters we deal with every day, we fall back on what we know are sloppy categories: hawks and doves, liberals and conservatives, hardliners and pragmatists...."[34]

Hence, President Reagan's 1981 legislation to cut income tax rates and index tax brackets, coupled with defense budget increases and a reduction in the rate of growth of many domestic spending programs, became "Reganomics."

The herd instinct, in its various forms, is endemic to the news business. Keep this in mind if you are the spokesperson for your company. You may be asked the same leading question over and over, with the result that your patience will be strained. Take a deep breath if necessary, but answer the question calmly and patiently, as if it had never been asked before.

RECYCLED NEWS

Just because you thought you had disposed of a negative story with a positive response, don't think it has been consigned to the newspaper's morgue or the radio or television station's tape stacks. Lou Cannon, in *Reporting*, cites the case of a *Washington Post* article in 1974 about purported banking and stock activities of President Nixon's friend "Bebe" Rebozo. Many other media picked up the story and treated it as fresh information, yet much of it had appeared months before in Long Island's *Newsday*.

In 1978 a newspaper account appeared a few months after the public relations firm founded by Michael K. Deaver and me had signed a contract to conduct a U.S. information program for the Republic of China (Taiwan). It implied that because Ronald Reagan was also a client of the firm, we would somehow influence his views in favor of Taiwan. This was either disingenuous or lazy reporting. Reagan had been publicly supportive of the Republic of China (Taiwan) for many years. Yet the story was picked up by the wire services and repeated widely as if this fact were not known. We found ourselves answering questions about it for months.

During the 1980 presidential campaign, the story reappeared as if it had never been written before. Political reporters whom we expected to have some memory of the earlier story (and certainly an understanding of Reagan's well-known positions on China issues) asked us the same questions again, as if they were suffering from amnesia.

Cannon says, "Sometimes stories are recycled simply because reporters and editors fail to read their own newspapers as carefully as they should."[35] In addition to recycling, most newspapers keep a list of stories not used on a particular day and held over for possible use later. This is sometimes called the "in-type" list, and stories with extended time value are called "evergreen." Television networks and stations do the same thing, shooting footage that is timeless and can be used whenever the editor needs to illustrate a story. When these stories appear in print or on the air they seem timely. It is the appearance of newness that counts, and if the information appears to be exclusive, it satisfies the editor's imperative to get the story and get it first.

OBJECTIVE REPORTING

More than 100 years ago the so-called objective reporting approach was on the rise. Ultimately, it came to dominate American journalism and still does.

The basic tenets of objective reporting are that the reporter must stick to the observable, verifiable facts; must include both sides in a controversy; and must not let personal beliefs and biases interfere with the narrative.

In theory, it seems fair. In practice, objective reporting has weaknesses. One is the widespread use by journalists of unidentified sources to build their stories. If the sources make accusations prefaced by phrases such as "sources say" or "critics say," it is very difficult for the accused to counter them effectively. As Cannon puts it, "...denials are no more a match for accusations than they were 25 years ago."[36]

Journalists sometimes defend such a practice by invoking the claim that they "can't play God." This begs the question of whether the reporter shares responsibility for harm to the subject of a story if accusations by others are reported and turn out to be false.

How can objective reporting, subject to manipulation and too reliant on unidentified sources, be improved? Cannon says that fairness is a better guideline for a reporter to follow than "objectivity." The latter, with its presumed neutrality, may lead reporters to overlook biases, both in their sources and themselves.

THE MEDIA VS. THEMSELVES

In 1970, then Vice President Spiro Agnew delivered his famous speech excoriating the media as "nattering nabobs of negativism." A 1983 survey by Professor Michael J. Robinson, director of the media analysis project at The George Washington

University, Washington, D.C., found that quite a lot of "nattering" was directed *at* the media *by* the media.

Robinson proceeded to find out how the media covered the media by monitoring and tallying all the relevant coverage in the *New York Times, Washington Post, Wall Street Journal, Time, Newsweek, U.S. News & World Report,* and the national evening news programs of ABC, CBS and NBC during a 13-week period. In the newspapers, he limited himself to coverage in the main news section, setting aside feature sections. He also excluded stories about foreign news media, Hollywood and telecommunications policy.

The survey led Robinson to two important conclusions: (1) the media consistently emphasize bad news about one another; (2) they are self-interested in their coverage, with print media knocking broadcast (and vice versa), and national media knocking regional and local media.

Robinson classified each story as "neutral," "good press" or "bad press." He said, "Reporters, columnists and editors produced an image of the press that was so disproportionately negative, no reasonable classification scheme could have failed to uncover it."[37]

What he found was this: 47 "bad press" stories and only 16 "good press" stories. Even with "neutral" stories added to the "good press" list, the combination added up to only half the stories tallied.

According to Robinson, the most fully covered media story during the period from January through April 1983 was one from Jacksonville, Alabama in which a local television camera crew filmed a man attempting self-immolation. This story had to be considered overwhelmingly "bad press" for the media, especially television, for it called into question journalists' ethics and taste.

In April 1983, when Gen. William Westmoreland won a skirmish in his legal battle with CBS over its documentary, "The Uncounted Enemy: A Vietnam Deception," both ABC and NBC covered the story on their evening news programs the same night. CBS did not say a word about it until two weeks later. Even then, it covered the story only tangentially.

Robinson says, "As a rule, neither CBS nor any other medium played up its own problems....each hyped the other guy's problems or downplayed its own."[38]

Despite the apparent relish of one medium for criticizing another, Robinson did not find a large number of media stories. Over the 13-week period of his survey there were only 93 stories—about one a day.

Negativism of the media toward one other has probably contributed to the demise of America's Media High. Robinson concludes that "if the news media cover themselves negatively, the public will tend to believe what it sees, hears or reads about the press, whatever the reality of the press happens to be."[39]

MUZZLE THE MEDIA?

Although Professor Robinson concluded that public skepticism toward the media is healthy, media people fret about it. Fret or not, media executives are getting rhetorical doses of medicine with increasing frequency from business executives.

Herbert Schmertz, vice president of public affairs of the Mobil Corporation, provided an example of the new willingness of business executives to talk back when he addressed a meeting of Gannett News Service executives:

> My hope is that those of you in positions of responsibility in the media will recognize that these [public] concerns are real and that they are damaging the viability of our free press and threatening our institutions. You may disagree as to the correctness of the reasons the public has for these concerns, but you will be wrong if you conclude that because you disagree, the concerns should be dismissed. Make no mistake about it—the concerns are real, and they are growing. Dismissal of them, because you either reject their accuracy, or because you believe the First Amendment gives you the right to turn a blind eye to

them, would be massively counter-productive because it would increase the hostility that portions of the public hold toward you.[40]

Schmertz said the media needed to examine three areas of criticism:

> First is a feeling that the press is simply too powerful. The public feels that the press is attempting to use its power not to report information but to make policy.
>
> The second source of concern by the public stems from a feeling that what they see and read regarding our leaders and institutions is substantially different from reality. The public does not believe that the leaders of our institutions and our government are really as dumb or corrupt as they appear in the press. Nor do they believe the institutions of our society are as rotten and uncaring as they are portrayed.
>
> The third area of concern is the public's view that the press, on occasion, uses practices which are abusive, unfair or unethical. The public knows that the press has the ability, and on occasion exercises that ability, to accuse, indict, prosecute, convict and punish an individual or an institution with a severity that exceeds any court.[41]

Schmertz's indictment of media excesses did not stop with these three specific concerns. He also said that we may be experiencing a sort of Gresham's law of journalism, "a situation where bad journalism has driven good journalism out of the market place....the public is now saying: 'You've gone too far—you are unfairly damaging reputations and credibility solely for financial gain.'"[42]

He also took sharp issue with the practice of reporters relying on unidentified sources. He told the Gannett executives:

> I have seen articles containing 15 or more sources, all unnamed....Descriptions such as 'a Wall Street analyst,' 'a knowledgeable broker,' or 'a business economist' were used. Yet if the public has the right to know, it has the right to evaluate the motivation, credibility and competence of a source,

particularly when that source is used to illustrate or document adverse information about an individual or institution. But just the opposite seems to be occurring. More and more unnamed sources are being used and the public is becoming more and more dubious as to their reliability if not their existence.

Are Schmertz's assertions just those of a corporate officer tired of having his company's activities and motives questioned, and irritated by widespread negativism in the media, or is he reflecting a widespread view? The results of two surveys by the Public Agenda Foundation suggest that the media elite believe that criticism of the media is widespread and stems less from legitimate concerns than from intolerance.

The surveys, conducted in 1979 and 1980, studied two groups. One consisted primarily of leading journalists, editors, publishers and interest group leaders. The second represented general public opinion. About the first group, the researchers said, "Many decision makers believe that Americans are essentially intolerant and reject freedom of expression."[43]

The "leadership" group cited a 1979 instance in a Maine high school in which 74 percent of the students in an 11th grade civics class signed a petition to repeal the Bill of Rights. The group also cited a 1970 poll broadcast on CBS' "60 Minutes," in which a majority of Americans rejected five out of 10 of the provisions of the Bill of Rights. Also cited was an incident in 1970 when some Massachusetts high school students asked more than 1,000 adults to sign the First Amendment as a petition to Congress. Fewer than half were willing to do so.

The researchers concluded that these media and interest group leaders think there is a gulf between themselves and the general public, with the latter believed to have little understanding or tolerance for the concept of freedom of expression. According to the researchers, the leaders think the public's hostility is rooted in "indefensible non-principles such as ignorance, intolerance, or a desire to 'shoot the messenger' who brings bad news."[44]

If this view is, indeed, widely held by the media elite, criticisms of the kind made by Herb Schmertz are likely to fall on deaf ears. But just how accurate is this dark assessment of public attitudes by the decision makers?

In the second of its surveys, the Public Agenda Foundation interviewed a random sample of 1,000 people, a cross section of the general public. It is clear from the results that it is *fairness* the public wants most from the news media. The public is far from intolerant, according to results of the survey:

♦ 61 percent believe communists have a right to say what they think on a television talk show. Only 29 percent were opposed

♦ 57 percent said that homosexuals have a right to get newspaper coverage to argue against laws they feel are discriminatory. Opposed: 31 percent

♦ 59 percent said that members of the Nazi party have a right to publish their own newspaper. Thirty percent were opposed

The general public group surveyed made a sophisticated distinction between freedom of expression and "deliberate provocation," by agreeing 62 to 26 percent that the Nazis do not have a right to stage a march through a predominantly Jewish neighborhood. In sum, their view was that Nazis have a right to be heard by publishing a newspaper, but not to cause trouble.

On the other hand, the public group surveyed wants nothing to do with peremptory antimedia actions. When asked if the president of the United States has the right to close down a newspaper that prints stories he feels are biased or inaccurate, 69 percent said no, and only 22 percent agreed.

The researchers concluded, "For the public, fair objective news reporting is more than an abstract ideal; it meets a very real, practical need. People believe that they will not have an accurate basis on which to make decisions, such as voting, unless they have access to news that provides all the information they need."[45]

The message from all quarters seems clear: If the media were to accentuate fairness instead of negativism, business and public criticism would decline. Let us assume, however, that this idyllic state will not come about any time soon. Meanwhile, you and your organization are faced with dealing with things as they are. Part Two is designed to help you do it successfully.

Part Two
DEALING WITH THE MEDIA

3/ How to Be Interviewed

Despite obvious differences between such news media as newspapers and television, there are some interview techniques common to all media. Special things you will need to know about being interviewed on television or for print media will be covered in the chapters on those media. This chapter, however, is intended to help you understand the interview techniques common to most journalism—from small-circulation newsletters to television networks—and how to deal with them.

First, remember the reporters' imperative: get the story. They and their editors or producers assume there is a story or they would not be interviewing you. You can help them get that story in a way that is positive and not damaging to you and your organization if you avoid: (1) self-inflicted verbal wounds, and (2) certain traps that may be set for you.

KEEPING IT SIMPLE

Every business and profession has its own jargon. Titles of programs that are a few words long become shortened to the program's initials. For example, to executives in the savings and loan business, the Federal Savings and Loan Insurance Corporation is referred to as the F.S.L.I.C. or even "Fizzlic." In your field, you and your colleagues talk in a sort of oral shorthand. This is a practical thing to do when people who share a common base of information on a particular subject are dealing with one another. To refer to everything by its full name would be tedious and unnecessary, if not downright silly. When you step out of your work environment, however, everything changes. When you are interviewed, you must assume that the interviewer does not know the technical jargon of your business.

In taking on the role of teacher, explain the whys and wherefores of your field, keep your explanations simple but not condescending. Treat the reporter as an adult. If you talk down to a print media reporter you risk negative treatment in the story that follows. If you do it on the air—on radio or television—you risk alienating the audience as well. If you want to persuade the audience of the rightness of your position on an issue, the audience must like you. They cannot do this if they do not understand what you are talking about.

A case in point. New York public relations executive Marvin Gurgold related this incident in an interview in *Frequent Flyer* magazine in July 1984: "Business executives tend to be so involved in their own arena that they find it difficult to articulate a message in very simple, easy-to-understand language. Doctors and lawyers especially tend to be in love with shoptalk. And once

I coached an educator who kept using the term 'primarily modular learning environment.' When I asked her what that meant, she said, 'classroom.'"

THE INTERVIEWEE'S RIGHTS

As the subject of an interview in either print or broadcast media, you have certain rights that are tacitly understood by the person conducting the interview. These are your rights to:

1. set ground rules;
2. select the topics to be covered;
3. change the subject;
4. ask questions yourself.

Ground rules include the length of the interview and whether or not it is to be "on the record." If your time is limited, let the interviewer know in advance rather than cut him or her off abruptly in mid-interview with a hasty, "I've got to go to another appointment now."

If you want to limit the topics, also let the interviewer know in advance. There may be a subject he or she wants to cover that you are not prepared to discuss. While it is your right to limit the range of topics to be covered, your inability to discuss a particular subject may render the session useless from the interviewer's point of view. If this is to happen, it is better to know it in advance rather than waste both the interviewer's time and yours.

Once the interview begins, you have a right to change the subject. If a particular question appears to be leading into an area you want to avoid or de-emphasize, you can give an abbreviated answer and make a bridge to a related subject that you do want to emphasize. The interviewer may come back to the question you did not fully answer, asking it in other ways. If so, keep bridging back to variations of the changed-subject reply you used the first time.

Answering a question with a question is one way to shift the focus of an interview. The following example puts you in the shoes of an officer of a public utility that operates a nuclear power plant:

> INTERVIEWER: Your plant has been shut down for safety reasons three times in the last 12 months. Aren't you concerned about an accident on the order of Three Mile Island? Are the risks of radioactivity escaping into the atmosphere acceptable to you?
>
> YOU: Safety regulations are stringent and we follow them carefully. The shutdowns were brief and the plant has a clean bill of health. As to risks, I think you are asking a larger question and that is, is nuclear energy too risky to use at all? Let me ask *you* a question: Given the fact that nuclear plants cannot explode, can you say that the remote chance of a core meltdown is a risk that is any greater than the health hazards of switching all power generation to coal, with the attendant air pollution?

HUMOR—HANDLE WITH CARE

During an interview, remember at all times that you are not engaged in casual conversation with an old friend. You are speaking, directly or indirectly, to a large audience. Be especially cautious if the interview seems to be going very well and the atmosphere is relaxed and cordial. You may be tempted to use humor, even flippancy. Forget it. Chances are, you will deliver yourself a wound you will regret. It is one thing to be good-natured in your interview, but quite another to bring off real humor. As the following examples show, the old adage "One man's meat is another's poison" is still true.

Geraldine Ferraro, after promising to release her income tax returns and her husband's during her vice presidential campaign in August 1984, later had to explain that her husband had declined to release his. She tried to explain his reluctance with a humorous remark: "You people married to Italian men, you know what it's like." Until then, the candidate had cultivated an image of determined independence. With this one remark, she conjured up two negatives: (1) Women married to men of Italian ancestry are submissive and dutiful; (2) men of Italian ancestry are stubborn and unreasonable.

New York Governor Mario Cuomo was one man of Italian ancestry who was not amused. He was quoted by the *New York Times* on August 15 as saying, "It didn't play well. It's not good to use ethnic stereotypes. It almost always gets you in trouble."

In Washington, a senior officer of a large public relations and lobbying firm made what he must have thought was a funny remark to a *Washington Post* reporter, but that came out sounding like a cynical comment on the public relations business. He said his firm might take as a client "a Communist government if one of those Eastern European ones [asks]. It's a business. We're mercenaries."[46]

OVERCONTROL

If you attempt to exert too much control over the circumstances in which you or your colleagues are interviewed, you may risk another self-inflicted wound. Consider this example.

The 1984 Summer Olympic Games in Los Angeles, despite their ultimate success, were the subject of controversy on and off during the period leading up to the events themselves.

To keep control over media relations, Peter Ueberroth, president of the Los Angeles Olympic Organizing Committee (LAOOC), established a policy of having an LAOOC news department representative monitor all interviews by LAOOC executives. The aides took notes, with the result that interviews were almost certainly less candid than they otherwise would have been. Was this device, with its overtones of intimidation, worth the risk? Probably not, when you consider that it was duly reported in a long article about Ueberroth by Bella Stumbo in the Los Angeles *Times*:

> ...it isn't easy to find out what they (LAOOC employees) honestly do think... Community relations officer John Bevilaqua, for instance, only looked frustrated when asked what he thought of Ueberroth's leadership. 'Oh, I don't want to get into that,' he said, glancing at the monitor, who promptly wrote it down.u24u27

TRICK QUESTIONS

A skillful interviewer may employ any of several verbal devices to put you on the spot. These trick questions will trap you if you are not familiar with the techniques and have not thought out answers in advance that will not only neutralize the questions, but will also turn them to your advantage.

Media training at the hands of professionals will sharpen your ability to deal with trick questions. Whether or not you have had such training, however, keep in mind three often used trick-question types: the Loaded Preface, the Either/Or Question and the Pregnant Pause.

Shirley Richard, head of corporate communications for the Adolph Coors Company, gave examples of these in an interview with the *Denver Post*. She was discussing preparations for a "60 Minutes" interview with the brewing company's head men, Bill and Joe Coors, in 1982.

Recounting the professional media training sessions the Coors brothers underwent, she pointed out that the trainers emphasized trick questions and how to bridge over from them to one of Coors' five communications objectives.

She gave this sample of the Loaded Preface: "Your business is slipping, there's an effective national boycott against you, people say you're anti-black, anti-woman. How can you expect to survive."[48]

Richard said the correct response would be, "I don't agree with your statements, but we will survive because we brew a unique quality beer."[49]

With the Either/Or question, selection of either one offered by the interviewer will put the interviewee in hot water. Here is the example Shirley Richard gave: "Your business is declining. Is it due to the boycott or to low employee morale?"[50] She offered this answer to the hypothetical question: "Neither. Vicious lies have had an impact, but getting the truth to the public about the quality of our beer and what a great place to work Coors is will change that."[51]

The Pregnant Pause—a trick-question device used largely on television—may be the most dangerous of the three. Picture yourself having just answered the interviewer's question succinctly and positively. Momentarily you feel good, satisfied at the quality of your answer. Yet the interviewer says nothing. There is no follow-up question, no new question, no nod, no sound. A second or two seems to stretch into minutes, then hours. The lights beat down on you; the camera's red eye bores in. You feel compelled to fill the emptiness. That is what the interviewer wants you to feel. He or she is using the Pregnant Pause to get you to extend your answer, to overanswer the original question, to put your foot in your mouth, thus opening up a new line of questioning. If you fill the Pregnant Pause you will probably regret it. Instead of doing that, look the interviewer in the eye earnestly, leaning forward a bit, just as you did when you answered the question. And smile. Don't grin just smile until he or she picks up the thread of the questioning again. Above all, don't flinch. If you do, you will blurt out a comment that will almost certainly put you on the defensive.

THE FOUR DEFENSES

Chances are you will never face the kind of grilling that a politician faces as a result of a verbal gaffe, accusations of unjustified junketing, or questionable campaign contributions or a skeleton in the closet. But if you find yourself on the defense in an interview, you may find that variations on the politician's four classic defenses are worth remembering:

1. I didn't do it.
2. I did it, but there was a good reason (explain).
3. I did it. I'm sorry. I was wrong and I've learned from my mistake. (Example: former U.S. Sen. Charles Percy's much-publicized *mea culpa* to Illinois conservative voters late in his 1978 reelection campaign.)
4. Whoever says I did such a thing is a low-down, good-for-nothing bum (or similar epithet). Follow this with a counterattack on your accuser—if you have the facts to back it up.

CONCLUSIONS

All of the suggestions in this chapter have one purpose: to help you put your best foot forward in an interview. Each of them rests on the assumption that you will invest time in thinking out the interview process and will carefully identify your communications objectives in advance. If you have clearly identified your objectives and worked them into summary statements, you will be much better able to handle any interview questions. Still, you and your colleagues should work out a list of questions you expect to be asked, and rehearse your answers. Do this not long before the interview, so the probable questions and answers will be fresh in your mind and your confidence level will be high.

There is no substitute for preparation before an interview. The interviewee who goes into the encounter expecting to wing it is usually in for a surprise, and not a pleasant one. Your interviewer will be well prepared. Can you afford not to be?

4/ Television: Making the Eye Work for You

For more than 20 years, a steadily growing majority of Americans have depended on television as their main source of news. Television, with its intimacy, its seductive "coolness" and its reputation as *the* impressionistic medium, has changed the way we think about events and sometimes even the events themselves. If you can master its uses you will have gone a long way toward mastering the other media as well.

It is now thought that television's nightly presentation of the horrors of war in Vietnam had a lot to do with turning American public opinion against the war. Plausible, too, is the view that television's dramatic depiction of any and all troubles at nuclear power plants has intensified public fears of nuclear power and, indirectly, contributed to construction delays and cost increases.

TV-THE PRIMARY NEWS SOURCE

Since 1959, the Roper Organization, Inc. has conducted regular public opinion polls for the Television Information Office on attitudes about the various news media.[52]

Compare the percentages in the answers to the question, "I'd like to ask you where you usually get most of your news about what's going on in the world today—from newspapers or radio or television or magazines or talking to people or where?" (multiple answers were permitted):

	1959	1982
Newspapers	57%	44%
Television	51	65
Radio	34	18
Magazines	8	6
People	4	5

More significant is a medium's credibility with its audience. Another of Roper's questions over the course of the years 1959 to 1982 has been, "If you got conflicting or different reports of the same news story from radio, television, the magazines and the newspapers, which of the four versions would you be most inclined to believe—the one on radio or television or in magazines or newspapers?" This question did not permit multiple answers. The results:

	1959	1982
Newspapers	32%	22%
Television	29	53
Radio	12	6
Magazines	10	8
Don't know/No answer	17	11

The dramatic rise in television's influence is reflected in the way people think of it as a community institution. In the polls,

Roper also asked respondents to rate local institutions on the quality of the job they do in the community. The rating choices were "excellent," "good," "fair," "poor." Combined ratings of "excellent" and "good" showed these rankings."

	1959	1982
Television	59%	70%
Schools	64	50
Local government	44	39

If television is so highly regarded at the community level, how fairly does it treat various groups? Roper asked his poll respondents if certain groups were treated fairly, too favorably or too unfavorably. While half thought the elderly were portrayed fairly, 36 percent felt they were treated too unfavorably. Business executives, on the other hand, received one of the lower treated fairly ratings, 48 percent. Yet 28 percent thought business people were treated too favorably. Lawyers were rated as being "treated fairly" by 47 percent, but too favorably by 35 percent. The figures for doctors were 49 and 39 percent, respectively.

The message here for business and professional people is this: If you think your field of endeavor is poorly treated on television, don't look to the viewers for sympathy. A lot of them may think you are already getting a break. Indeed, this means you must work doubly hard when you go on television to establish a credible presence for yourself and your point of view.

SON OF MEDIA HIGH?

In Chapter One, the phenomenon of America's Media High was examined, along with the conclusion that the days of reporters and media personalities being treated as heroes were over. The collective public cheering at the government's decision to keep reporters from joining the Grenada landings in October 1983 was the sharpest evidence that the Media High was over.

Why then does television rate so well in the Roper surveys? Is another Media High on the way?

No. The seeming contradiction can be explained by the nature of the medium of television. While there is widespread public disenchantment with what is seen as the overly powerful and "arrogant" media, this feeling tends to be generalized and it does not negate television's potency. This potency is a factor of what the late Marshall McLuhan, the Canadian media scholar and analyst, called television's "coolness."

McLuhan divided all media into "hot" and "cool." For him a hot medium is one of "high definition"—that is, one filled with data. As examples, he cited photographs (high definition because they provide so much detailed information) versus cartoons (low definition because one's imagination must fill in so much information). Your daily newspaper is a hot medium because it is packed with information and leaves little to your imagination. Television, on the other hand, is cool because it conveys constantly changing images and creates impressions that allow for a wide range of interpretations by individual viewers. McLuhan said that "hot media are...low in [audience] participation, and cool media are high in participation or completion by the audience."[53]

How Reagan Uses TV's Coolness

In *Understanding Media*, McLuhan says that "TV is a medium that rejects the sharp personality and favors the presentation of processes rather than of products."[54]

Richard Nixon, who was uncomfortable on television, often expressed a preference for radio. This is probably because his personality came across as sharp and negative on television. Ronald Reagan, on the other hand, probably understands better than any other public figure today how best to use television's coolness. He understands, as McLuhan put it, that television favors "the presentation of processes." He has demonstrated his mastery of the medium many times. One of the most vivid was the televised debate with then President Jimmy Carter in October 1980.

Carter's people (who never did understand television) were certain, going into the debate, that their chief's encyclopedic knowledge of the issues would overwhelm Reagan who, they thought, would put his foot in his mouth. They were certain that Carter would win the debate. Indeed, a number of print media reporters in the debate audience declared Carter the winner. This is not surprising, for these reporters were watching a platform debate and the rest of America was participating in an intimate television experience. Also, because print media reporters work in the environment of an information-packed hot medium, many of them do not understand the rival medium, television. Indeed, some seem preoccupied with disdaining television rather than understanding it.

Reagan has communicated effectively on television for years, understanding both its impression-creating quality and its intimacy. He realized long ago that when you face the television camera you are talking not to millions but to one person sitting in his or her living room—multiplied millions of times.

In the debate with Carter, Reagan's objectives were clear and uncomplicated. He needed to convey the impression that he was likable, capable and would not embroil the nation in a war. And that was the impression he gave.

Carter, on the other hand, was intense and, at several times during the debate, sharply critical of Reagan. The impression he gave was that of a man both nervous and nasty. Since his competence as president had already become an issue with the public, his image of personal decency was one of his few remaining campaign assets. By turning on Reagan he undercut his own asset. When, after one of these bursts of Carter criticism, Reagan turned to his opponent and said, "There you go again," he reinforced his own air of gentle reason. Indeed, at that moment, many think, Reagan won the debate hands down.

Carter and his people treated television as if it were a sort of animated newspaper, a medium in which the debater who dispenses the greater amount of detailed factual data will carry the day. Reagan, although he was well prepared on the issues, knew that the impressions the debaters created in the minds of the television viewers would have a lasting impact, while a barrage of "facts" would not. The impact of the different impressions created by the two men had a direct effect on the outcome of the election.

Media consultant Walter Pfister tested the facts-versus-impressions thesis on four business executives who watched the televised debate with him. Pfister's theory, quoted by journalist Rudy Maxa, is that "audiences are won by the *attitudes* of the candidates."[55] To test his belief, at the end of the debate Pfister asked his four guests to choose the most important thing Carter and Reagan had each said. One man told Pfister that he liked the way Reagan shook hands. Another noted that Carter didn't seem very presidential, that he seemed ill at ease. Another said he liked the way Reagan had chided Carter with the gentile admonition, "There you go again, Mr. President."

Pfister's point was: "They didn't answer my question about what the candidates had said—they gave me their *impressions*. And the unanimous impression was that, in a contest between Carter and Reagan, Reagan had It."[56]

TV, the Close-up Medium

Marshall McLuhan contended that television is a close-up medium. We, the audience, tend to identify with the life of the character the television actor is portraying. In the case of film stars, on the other hand, it is the trappings of the star's real life that interest us. He cites a study of young school children who wore head cameras while watching television. Consistently, the children concentrated on the reactions of the actors to actions and events, as if they were the actors themselves.

McLuhan cites an interview with actress Joanne Woodward in which she was asked the difference between being a movie star and a television actress. She replied, "When I was in the movies I heard people say, 'There goes Joanne Woodward.' Now they say, 'There goes somebody I think I know.'"[57]

Because television viewers are so involved with the medium, they are, in effect, participants in it. McLuhan argues that television is really an extension of our sense of touch. If so, that may explain TV's great popularity with politicians who, if they could, would individually touch each potential voter to create a bond of intimacy. Lacking that possibility, they turn to the most intimate substitute, television. And those like Ronald Reagan who know how to use it use it very effectively.

Shaping Impressions: The Adelman Case

Television can create impressions where information-filled hot media, such as newspapers, cannot. Take the case of Kenneth Adelman and his January 1983 Senate confirmation hearings as director of the U.S. Arms Control and Disarmament Agency (ACDA).

Adelman, who had been a scholar-researcher with the Stanford Research Institute (SRI) in Washington, D.C., and later deputy to U.S. Ambassador to the United Nations Jeane Kirkpatrick, had been nominated for the ACDA position by President Reagan. The nomination put Adelman right into the middle of a holy war between the doves—those committed to arms control—and the hawks, who believe that arms control negotiations cannot succeed unless U.S. defenses are first rebuilt and negotiations proceed from a position of strength.

Adelman was seen by the first group as representing the views of the latter group, a not unreasonable assumption since the latter group's views reflect those of Reagan and his administration. The doves had great misgivings about Adelman—or any hawk—serving as the nation's chief arms control official. They began to prepare for a major assault on the nomination in the Senate Foreign Relations Committee, whose duty it was to recommend (or not recommend) Adelman for a confirmation vote of the entire Senate.

The Reagan administration had decided that Adelman should

be low-keyed in his replies to the senators' questions in order not to turn the nomination hearing into a media donnybrook on the larger arms control issue. The Republicans had the votes, after all, but network television almost changed all of that.

Early in the hearing, Senator Claiborne Pell (a Democrat from Rhode Island) asked Adelman whether, if a nuclear war started, it could be contained. This was a leading question since, to those in the arms control camp, it is an article of faith that the first nuclear explosion would lead to a series of exchanges that would wipe out civilization.

Network television carried the first part of Adelman's answer that evening: "Senator Pell, I just have no thoughts in that area...." What the networks did not carry was the rest of Adelman's answer: "...and I will tell you why. I think it would be such a time of extreme human stress and extreme conditions that I think any predictions on what leaders around the world would do in that kind of situation would just not be accurate or not be based on anything that I know."

With the second half of the statement left on the cutting room floor, Adelman was made to appear ignorant and unqualified. Adelman recalls the hearing that Thursday this way:

> There were 30 to 50 reporters there. Associated Press, UPI, the [New York] *Times*, the [Washington] *Post*, the *Christian Science Monitor*. All the major [print] ones—reported that the hearing had some rough sledding but that my confirmation would go through. No one reported any 'I don't knows' or that I was ignorant. On network television, however, that was what came across. I checked the transcript later. I said, 'I don't know' six times out of a total of 86 questions.
>
> By Sunday, the very same people who had attended the hearing and reported on it were writing that my testimony was a disaster and that my confirmation was in big trouble. Nothing had changed in the meantime except that the television coverage had focused on the 'I don't knows.'[58]

Adelman was confirmed ultimately, but when he reflected about what he had gone through during those days, he said,

"When you have people who experience a phenomenon, then watch it on television, television becomes the reality and their own experience gets wiped out."[59]

Had the television editors snipped the film or tape because they were arms control doves or because the "I don't knows" made a sharper, more controversial story in a 20-second sequence on the evening news? Probably the latter, although we will never know for sure. The incident underscores the *process* aspect of television. The print media reporters became actors—not just reporters—in the process, as a result of television's treatment of the story. The film editor set the process in motion; impression did the rest.

TOO MUCH POWER?

Even high-level policy makers can be caught up in the television process. Lloyd N. Cutler, counsel to the president in the Carter administration and now a Washington lawyer, brought no rival-media bias to the table when, in an interview on C-SPAN, the Washington-based public affairs cable TV system, he commented on the great power of television to shape events. He described how surprised he had first been to find how much media deadlines, especially those of the television evening news programs, affected the White House. He cited this example:

> ...If something happened, let us say, on a Monday, or somebody strongly criticized the President, or the Russians did something...everything stopped! Whatever you'd been working on as the great priority of the next morning you had to put aside in order to reach a decision about how the President or someone else would respond in time for the television evening news.
>
> The notion that there wouldn't be any response at all, or that you were going to wait and think about it before you came to a decision always got overcome by the need to say something and avoid a rerun of the criticism of action of the day before, or a

story that the President's aides are divided or that he can't decide what to do. The President is supposed to come out looking strong and decisive even if he's just acted on the spur of the moment. And that's the galvanizing force of that evening news.[60]

TURNING GOOD NEWS TO BAD

If TV is such a galvanizing force, can it actually turn good news to bad? When it comes to the state of the economy, President Reagan thinks it can. In one of his weekly radio broadcasts (March 10, 1984) he said that while the economic recovery had moved forward in the second half of 1983, "the coverage on network television was still in recession."

Reagan singled out the TV networks as a result of a study of their economics news coverage by the Institute for Applied Economics (IAE), a New York-based research group. During 1983, the IAE conducted a six-month, seven-nights-a-week survey of economics stories on ABC, CBS and NBC.

The IAE examined three questions about network coverage:

1. Did the networks fully report the news of the economic recovery?
2. Did the networks bias their reporting to play down the positive impact of the economy?
3. Did the networks use negative case studies to detract from the generally positive news?

Holmes M. Brown, president of the institute, contends that the networks turned good news into bad "by concentrating on the pockets of recession within the overall recovery, thereby implying that behind the good news of falling inflation and rising employment there were black clouds of economic misery."[61]

He cited several examples, including a U.S. Labor Department announcement, July 8, 1983, of a drop in unemployment. The CBS report of this, by correspondent James Brady, emphasized the number still unemployed and focused on worsening unemployment in certain states. The good news was not the focus of the CBS coverage.

In December, when another drop in unemployment was announced, ABC emphasized not that good news, but concentrated on those who still sought jobs, interviewing two businessmen who had been out of work for a year and a half. Brown says, "A story that began with a 0.3 percentage drop in unemployment ended in complete despair and talk of suicide."[62]

When the government announced that the gross national product had grown at a vigorous 7.7 percent rate for the third quarter of 1983, the IAE study showed that NBC economics editor Irving R. Levine, on the October 22 network news, focused on pockets of poverty instead.

On July 15, when ABC reported that factory production had risen sharply from May to June, anchor Max Robinson hurried by the good news to note, "However, the economic changes triggered by the recession continued." This led to a long story about the closing of an International Harvester plant.

Whether it is seeing the small dark cloud behind good news or whether it is a matter of drawing you into a controversy by getting you to respond to someone's criticism or accusations, the television reporter's imperative is to get a vivid—and brief—story on the news.

MAKING TELEVISION WORK FOR YOU

According to Anne Ready, a Los Angeles-based media consultant, Richard Nixon only made things worse for himself when he said on television, "I am not a crook." Ready, whose firm, Ready for Media, has a diversified clientele of major corporations and public relations firms, says that Nixon broke a basic rule in the use of the medium with that statement. The rule: Don't repeat your accuser's allegations.

This rule has a corollary, which is: be positive. "If Nixon had said, 'I'm honest,' instead of what he did say, 'I am not a crook'would not have become part of our folklore," Ready contends. This is consistent with what she tells her clients. She coaches them in what she calls "The Six Cs." She says that executives who find themselves on the business end of the camera's eye must learn to express themselves "concisely, candidly, conversationally, clearly, correctly and with compassion. Hence, the six Cs."

Have a SOCO

Not only did then President Nixon fuel the fire with his statement, he also failed to accomplish a SOCO. These are the initials for a Single Overriding Communications Objective. You will need a SOCO any time you face the media, according to Anne Ready. In Nixon's case, at the time, an appropriate SOCO would have been the calming of wavering supporters.

You can have two or three secondary points you want to get across in an interview, but they must serve the basic objective—the SOCO—in order to reinforce it.

Ready says the biggest mistake people make when they are interviewed on television is "waiting for the right question and not remembering their objective." Her point is that if you wait for the right question it will probably never come and, in any case, your interviewer will completely control the agenda of the interview.

In working with her clients, Ready says, "We get them to focus on their objective in mock interviews so they can use the actual television interview to their advantage. The best approach is to acknowledge the question, then 'bridge' to the answer that furthers your objective. An example of a 'bridge' is, 'I'm asked that question often, and the best way to answer it is————————,' followed by a statement that works toward your objective, your SOCO."[63]

Peter Jacobi, a former journalism teacher now a partner in Jack Hilton, Inc., another media consulting firm, says, "We teach that you shouldn't have to be slaves to questions....You don't evade them; you don't avoid them. But then, move to your own objectives."[64]

The following case has been disguised. It is based on an actual one that occurred in a western state several years ago. The questions and answers illustrate the way well-prepared executives avoid being slaves to the questions and move to their objectives.

The case: You are president of a supermarket chain. Your stores enjoy a good following. Your markets are clean, airy and well lit. Prices are competitive. Your employees have high morale. Suddenly, a random inspection turns up some packages of ground beef with traces of rat feces in them. The word quickly gets out. You are besieged by calls from the media. Your objective is to calm customer fears that other products might be contaminated and that ground beef from your stores will forever be suspect. The interview runs like this:

Q. Doesn't this incident raise questions about your quality control procedures, overall, on fresh food?

A. First let me tell you about the immediate steps we have taken to solve the problem. Fewer than 10 packages from one shipment from one of the three packing houses that supply us with meat appear to be involved. None of these packages had gone from our warehouse to our stores. There is no chance that any of the affected packages from this shipment can have been purchased by our customers. But we are going a step further. We have pulled every package of ground beef from previous shipments from our shelves. We will inspect every single one. None of these packages will go back on sale. Also, we are reviewing with each of our suppliers their quality control procedures. We won't accept any new shipments until we are satisfied that the problem won't be repeated.

Q. Yes, but if quality control is such that a few packages of bad beef can slip through, how can you be sure it won't happen with other meats or any fresh product?

A. We've been in business 25 years and during that time I guess we've sold close to a million pounds of ground beef without a single problem. I'm sorry this happened. It shouldn't have, and it won't happen again. Our quality control is very tight, but as soon as we've pinpointed this problem, it is going to be even tighter. Meanwhile, as I said, we are taking no chances and are pulling all the ground beef off our shelves. Furthermore, if any customer has any of our ground beef at home they can return it to the store and we will give them a refund, no questions asked.

In this case, the supermarket executive is, as he should be, forthright and open. He apologizes for the immediate problem without becoming defensive, and he spells out steps he has taken to solve it and calm consumer fears. Also, rather than answering the interviewer's first question directly, he moves immediately toward his objective by narrowing the dimensions of the problem. This is in line with the advice media consultants give their clients: Get to the bottom line first, then reinforce it with facts and examples. A variation on this, when your position is controversial and the other side is popular, is sometimes called...

Yes, We Have No Bananas

If you find yourself defending a complicated and unpopular position, state the positive aspects of your position first, avoiding negative statements about the other side. Prepare to hear yourself over and over again, for it may take you some time and much repetition before your message begins to take hold. This is especially true if your position requires detailed explanation in order to be well understood, and the other side's position can be easily summarized and benefits from oversimplification.

In the late 1970s, the American public was more or less evenly divided about the Equal Rights Amendment to the Constitution, although the pro-ERA view usually had a slight edge in public opinion polls. In any case, proponents of the amendment had succeeded in making it a litmus test for politicians about their commitment to equal rights for women. In their view, if you supported the amendment you were for equal rights; if you did not, you weren't. The news media, always looking for ways to simplify complicated issues, picked up the refrain.

Ronald Reagan, as a presidential candidate in 1976 and a likely one for 1980, was frequently asked his position on the ERA as he traveled the lecture circuit around the country. He was reluctant to support constitutional amendments in general and he was concerned about this one in particular because its wording was so broad that he believed it would, if ratified, bring on years of court tests for interpretation, thus turning judges into legislators.

For a time, Reagan, when asked by interviewers, "Do you support the Equal Rights Amendment?" would reply, "No," followed by his explanation that he thought there was a better way to achieve equal rights: changes and improvements in federal and state statutes. This invariably resulted in media reports that Reagan opposed the ERA, with his positive comments being lost on the cutting room floor. As long as his answer began with a negative, people stopped listening. This included the media, women's rights activists and worried Reagan supporters.

It worried his staff, too. We recommended that he rephrase his answer to the ERA question by putting the positive aspect of his position first. He did. Thus, the exchange would go this way:

Q. Do you favor the Equal Rights Amendment?
A. I support equal rights for women. The ERA is one approach. I think there is a better one. In recent years there have been some important changes in federal and state laws to insure equal pay for equal work and other rights for women. We need to look at our statutes to find out where discrimination against women still exists and change those that do. The ERA, on the other hand, would result in years of tangled court cases. We can solve the remaining equal rights questions much more quickly by changing any laws that stand in the way of equality.

The first benefit for Reagan in using this approach was that it foreclosed the go-for-the-jugular follow-on questions that had become a staple when he began his ERA answer with "No." If you find yourself, as he did, in a situation where the basic argument is over means and not goals and you are on the less popular side, do two things:

1. State your position in positive terms.
2. Don't feed the controversy.

Reporters are interested in propagating and extending controversy. That is a basic part of their business. When you state, up front, your agreement with the other side as to goals, but then disagree in a calm, conversational manner about ways to reach those goals, you drain much of the controversy and emotional charge from the issue.

To summarize: The two most important things you must bring to a television appearance are (1) your communications objective, ready to be stated succinctly; (2) a positive approach to your answers and statements. Now that you have these firmly in mind, let us turn to the physical aspects of your TV debut.

Looking Your Best

The key to looking your best on camera lies in one word: "simplicity." Maureen Pater Hanson, who has conducted media techniques workshops for national public relations firms, sets down this ground rule about dressing for television: "Wear dark colors (more authoritative); no wild colors or patterns such as stripes and plaids."
Other rules:

DO: (men)
Wear a solid light blue shirt.
Wear a dark-colored suit (blue or gray).

(women)
Wear a solid light blue blouse or women's shirt.
Wear a dark-colored suit or blazer.

DON'T: (men)
Wear striped shirts (they "dance" on camera).

Wear white shirts (they glare).
Wear jeweled tie tacks (they reflect light).
Wear gold chains or clunky ID braclets.
Wear wild-colored neckties.

(women)
Wear sparkling, glittery jewelry or noisy bracelets.
Wear large earrings.
Wear ruffles, narrow skirts or deep necklines—or anything else that makes you sit awkwardly and is distracting.

About eyeglasses, if you wear them, don't wear the (photosensitive) type that turn dark in the sun. If you do, the television lights will make you look like a *mafioso*.

On balance, the experts agree that your television attire should be neutral. "You don't want to draw undue attention to your clothes or distract from your message," says Hanson.

Eye Contact

It will be hard at first, but with practice you will be able to treat that cold camera's eye for what it really is: a window to that audience of one (multiplied many times) to whom you want to make your point.

More rules:

DO:

Look your interviewer in the eye most of the time.
Look straight at the camera's eye some of the time.
Look a fellow panelist in the eye if you are talking to him or her.
Make eye-contact changes from one place to another smoothly.
Behave as if the camera and sound system are always turned on.

DON'T:
> Look at the monitor screen.
> Look into the distance when someone else is talking. Watch them.
> Let your eyes wander or dart back and forth between the interviewer and the camera.

It is important that eye-contact transitions be made smoothly and deliberately and not too frequently. For example, you may be listening intently to the interviewer's questions, looking him or her in the eye. Pause to appear to ponder the question, then move your eye contact to the camera (the audience) before answering. The next time, keep your eyes on the interviewer when you answer the question.

When you are involved in a panel discussion, do not let your eyes wander when you are not directly involved in a question. It tells the audience you are bored.

The camera is on when the red light above the lens is lit. Many programs use two or even three cameras, and it is not possible to keep track constantly of which one is on without your eyes darting about. So, relax. At the end of the show the camera will still be rolling as credits are superimposed on the screen. Just keep on chatting with the host as if you were still on the air. The producer will let you know when they are finished. Meanwhile, "Don't do anything that you don't want seen at home by 100,000 people," says Michael Sheehan, a television coach for the Democratic National Committee.[65]

If you are new to television and expect to be doing a number of interviews, consider investing in some training sessions. By videotaping you in mock interview situations, the trainer can give you a detailed critique of your performance, and you can see for yourself where your eye contact needs improvement.

Posture

Here the rules are simple, but when you are trapped on a television set with those hot lights on you, the temptation to "get comfortable" may seem irresistible. Resist it.

DO:

Sit up straight (but not stiffly, which will make you seem dogmatic).

Keep your feet on the ground.

Keep your hands in your lap (or on the arms of the chair if they are low ones) when you are listening or being asked a question.

Lean forward slightly, using your hands for emphasis, when you want to get a point across.

DON'T:

Slouch or sink into the furniture.

Cross your legs.

Wave your arms wildly.

Swivel incessantly if you are in a swivel chair.

Strike an overly familiar or casual pose.

Nervous Smile

Media trainer Anne Ready says, "Business executives have a hard time smiling—at least many do. We try to put them in a relaxed situation and videotape them without their knowledge. Usually it involves just talking conversationally about the subject they know best: their business. Then I show them the videotape of this relaxed situation and compare it with a tape we have done of them in a mock interview. They see the difference immediately."

Until you have been before the cameras many times you will probably experience some apprehension and nervousness just prior to an interview. Television can be intimidating, but it need not be and will not be if you have learned to relax by seeing yourself on practice session videotapes.

The easiest way to eliminate nervousness is to learn to smile. If necessary, take a deep breath before you answer a question (but do it unobtrusively). This gives you a chance to "gather up" that smile.

It is especially important to smile if the interviewer seems hostile. This will reduce the intensity he or she is trying to build. It is hard to appear defensive if you are smiling.

Know Your Interviewer

"Don't go in the room thinking you're going to talk to a lamb, and there's a leopard in there," says media trainer Sheehan.[66] If you are not familiar with your television interviewer's style (or the nature of the audience if it is a talk show), study it. Watch the program or get a tape of it.

During the interview, address the interviewer or show host by his or her first name (but don't use the interviewer's name so often that you seem patronizing). This will tell the audience that you are calm and confident. This is particularly important if the interviewer is hostile and is addressing you as "Mr." or "Ms." It shows you aren't rising to the bait.

Sound Bites

A television interviewer gathering material for a news program is looking for a brief, pithy comment from you that will effectively augment his or her story. This is called a "sound bite." Is is usually about 20 seconds of sound on film or tape. As you develop your Single Overriding Communications Objective—SOCO—prior to being interviewed, think in terms of a brief answer that telegraphs your objective. If you have a sound bite ready, the interviewer will get a better story and you will get your point across.

The story is told of an oil company executive on a panel show during the 1979 gasoline shortage crisis. Toward the end of the program the host asked him to summarize, in 30 seconds, the solution to the problem. He began by saying, "First you have to understand the history of the oil industry...." Obviously, no one had told him about sound bites.

Next time you watch the evening TV news, time the stories. Most run under two minutes. Time the comments of those interviewed. Twenty seconds will begin to seem like a long time.

Faced with an interview, think about your sound bite in advance and test it on your colleagues and advisers. Do not leave it to chance. Off-the-cuff is usually off-the-mark.

What to Do If Mike Wallace Calls

Don't hang up. It probably will not be the star correspondent of "60 Minutes" himself, but a producer who will call. No matter. If "60 Minutes," "20-20," or your local investigative television reporter phones, take the call or have your public relations director take it to find out what is wanted. Don't have all your executives "in a meeting" or otherwise unavailable. Above all, do not give the impression your company is going to stonewall the investigators. That will only whet their appetites and heighten their suspicions.

Because there seem to be so many negative stories about business on the investigative shows, most executives are understandably apprehensive about the thought of getting a call from one of them. Arnold Zenker, a media coach, was interviewed by Mike Wallace for the "60 Minutes" segment about the work of media coaches, mentioned earlier in this book. Zenker made the point that, to most business executives, television is "a totally new world. They do not rise to a position of prominence in a corporation with a microphone in their hand or staring down the barrel of a camera." He noted that many senior executives are engineers or accountants by training, and, he told Wallace, when an investigative reporter calls to come see them, "...they're terrified of the apparatus, they're terrified of the lights, and they're terrified of you or your counterpart."[67]

Zenker agrees with other professionals in the field that the secret lies in helping investigative reporters do their job. "If you can speak in...an incisive way, in headlines, in 18 seconds you'll have a better chance of having a good result."[68] Sound familiar? It is communications objectives and sound bites again.

Helping reporters get a good story is just what the Adolph Coors Company did in 1982, and it reaped rewards for months afterward.

The Coors Case

It was Mike Wallace who called the Colorado brewing company one day in April 1982. When he was connected with John McCarty, the vice president for corporate public affairs, Wallace said, "Don't hang up."

Wallace had put in the call to Joe Coors to ask him about the long-running boycott of Coors beer. There had been charges of racial discrimination in hiring practices, searches of employees and abuse of preemployment lie detector tests. Coors was out, so McCarty got the call. After Wallace described the questions he had in mind, McCarty took a deep breath and urged him to travel to Golden, Colorado to get his story straight from the Coors brothers, Joe and Bill, and their employees.

McCarty had stuck his neck out. He talked with the brothers. Joe, at first, said "No," but discussions went on in the brewery's upper echelons, and five weeks later Mike Wallace and his crew were in Golden.

When Coors decided to let "60 Minutes" visit the brewery, it decided to go all the way. Wallace and his crew could examine any files and records, talk with any employee, go anywhere on the property. The Coors brothers and their executives decided that their best approach was to be completely open, that truth was on their side in their dispute with a union and other groups boycotting their beer.

Shirley Richard, head of Coors' corporate communications department, put the company's objective succinctly in an interview after the "60 Minutes" visit: "Most companies just want to survive '60 Minutes.' We wanted to do more than survive."[69]

Coors spent $60,000 on preparation for the "60 Minutes" visit, put several employees to work on research, and engaged a media training firm, Fairchild and Associates of Dallas, to prepare the Coors brothers.

Once the brothers had made the crucial decision to invite the "60 Minutes" crew in to roam at will and also to be interviewed themselves on camera, the entire company seemed to throw itself into the effort.

By the time "60 Minutes" covered the Coors story, the boycott had taken on a life—and lore—of its own. In addition to various unions, the boycott was joined by some black, student and gay groups. The word had been spread that Coors discriminated in its hiring practices and had poor employee relations. Few people knew the actual story behind the boycott, which began in 1977 as a union contract issue.

At that time, the brewery union went out on strike after Coors and it could not agree on terms of the contract. Within a month, most of the Coors workers were back on the job. Coors management contends that the issues were not major enough to sustain a walkout. The union, not surprisingly, claims that the workers could not go without paychecks, thus they were forced to return to work. Still, the fact is that 21 months after the strike, the workers voted to decertify the union by a 71- to 29-percent margin.

Coors management says the union was decertified because the brewery's wages and benefits are among the best in the region and that the workers neither wanted nor needed a union any longer. The union of course disagrees and has continued the boycott.

In the "60 Minutes" segment, it was the Coors point of view that seemed to carry the day. The union case, presented by spokesman David Sickler, came across as less persuasive, even strident in tone.

For Coors, preparation paid off. Shirley Richard, the corporate communications chief, organized the preparation plan and coordinated its execution. Coors did these things to get ready for "60 Minutes":

◆ Obtained and studied news stories about "60 Minutes"

◆ Reviewed videotapes of other "60 Minutes" pieces done by Coors segment producer Allan Maraynes. (Richard realized that the producer is the key element in an investigative story)

- ◆ Talked with other companies that had been subjects of Maraynes' pieces

- ◆ Reviewed tapes of speeches by Sickler, the union boycott leader. (Since "60 Minutes" uses a point-counterpoint technique in presenting slices of interviews, it was important to know what issues the other side would concentrate on)

- ◆ Compiled likely questions Mike Wallace would ask

- ◆ Developed a list of points Coors wanted to communicate. They were: (1) Coors is a good place to work; (2) the boycott is unfair and is carried on by a few rejected union officials; (3) Coors cares about its employees and its community; (4) Coors is not antiunion; (5) Coors makes a unique beer

- ◆ Arranged for media training for Bill and Joe Coors. (They learned how to spot trick questions and other techniques designed to make interviewees vulnerable and defensive)

Shirley Richard reminded the Coors brothers to keep calm and not to get angry with Wallace. She told them, "He can get hostile, but you can't." She warned them not to say things that might seem patronizing, such as "That's a good question, Mike." She also emphasized that they should use simple, direct language, "because the audience wasn't Mike Wallace, it was the viewers and beer drinkers."[70]

Richard and the crew from Fairchild and Associates, the media trainers, also instructed the Coors brothers on appearance and posture. Gone were Joe's photosensitive glasses. The chairs they were to sit in were carefully selected to be comfortable and also to encourage them to sit straight without appearing rigid.

As is customary in media training, the Fairchild crew taped the brothers in a mock interview situation in the actual room that would be used for the "60 Minutes" interview. They analyzed the videotape, then went through the questioning a second time. the training session lasted half a day.

The interview with Mike Wallace went well for Joe and Bill Coors. Lisa LeMaster, of Fairchild, attributed this to the fact that every question had been anticipated; the brothers were well prepared and thus relaxed on camera; and they had their objectives clearly in mind and articulated them clearly.

Just before the interview another event took place that cheered the brothers and their executives. Mike Wallace had been the guest, on camera, at a brown-bag lunch with several hundred Coors employees. It turned into a company pep rally. John McCarty introduced Wallace. After some opening remarks, Wallace asked for questions from the floor. Would "60 Minutes" tell the truth about this good company, they wanted to know. Would they talk with people other than the boycotters? Did Wallace like Coors beer, and would he take some home? And so it went.

Producer Maraynes concludes that the enthusiastic brown baggers were credible and actually reflected what he was hearing from others at the brewery. He said, "I thought, 'All the skeptics within the plant are going to see this, and they'll get angry and get in touch with us to tell us what was really going on.'"[71] But no one called.

The "60 Minutes" segment that aired turned out to be a major public relations plus for the Adolph Coors Company. Producer Maraynes, interviewed afterward, took the position that Coors' preparation was not the cause of the positive way the company came across on the air. His point was that if "60 Minutes" had had "the goods" on Coors, all that preparation would not have made any difference. True enough, but if you have the facts on your side, as Coors apparently did, poor preparation could result in a presentation far less positive and persuasive than the one that appeared on the air.

Indeed, Coors' careful preparation made it possible for the company to launch a comprehensive public relations campaign around the time of the "60 Minutes" airing. It went on for many months.

Here is a summary of the things Coors did to capitalize on the "60 Minutes" event:

- Had its own crew follow the "60 Minutes" crew, filming everything the other did

- Held an open house for all its employees, to show them the "60 Minutes" film

- Sent a thank-you letter to Mike Wallace on butcher paper—about 30 feet long—signed by hundreds of Coors employees

- Bought the noncommercial rights to the segment for $40,000, made more than 400 copies and sent one to each Coors distributor for showing to local service clubs and other groups

- Ran ads featuring pro-Coors editorials from local newspapers, under the heading "Thanks Neighbors!" and with the tag line, "Now that you know the truth, isn't it time to drink Coors?"

- Hired an audience-response-measuring firm that found that one of every five beer drinkers saw the program and had a positive reaction to the Coors message

- Sought a summer rerun of the "60 Minutes" segment. The criteria for a rerun are: (1) is it of continuing interest; (2) can it be updated; and (3) was the show a popular one? The answer to all three was "yes," and "60 Minutes" reran the segment on June 5, 1982

- When it learned the segment would be run again, Coors ran newspaper ads in 20 of its major markets, under the headline "The four most dreaded words in the English language: Mike

Wallace is here." Coors let "60 Minutes" know of its plans to run the ads. Maraynes told an interviewer that he knew of no other case where a company that had been the subject of a "60 Minutes" segment had run ads to draw attention to it

- Featured the program in its company newsletter, including a sampling of the more than 500 letters the brewery received after the program had aired

- Shirley Richard prepared a seminar with slides on the company's "60 Minutes" experience. Intended for college journalism classes (college students had been among the most ardent boycott suporters), the seminar was soon in heavy demand from other companies and public relations groups

- John McCarty delivered a lecture on "What to do when '60 Minutes' Calls" at a Boston university seminar, "The Economy, Business and the News Media"

After the "60 Minutes" airing of the Coors story, CBS producer Allan Maraynes told an interviewer that good investigative reporting leans to blacks and whites, not grays. In the Coors case, once the "60 Minutes" crew had satisfied itself that the allegations about Coors were unfounded, its editing seemed to reflect that conclusion. Thus, in the segment that aired to millions of television viewers, Coors seemed to be wearing the white hats while its adversary, the union, wore the black ones.

We turn now from the highest-profile medium to one that is not only invisible, but is also often overlooked by executives who need to communicate a message.

5/ Whatever Happened to Radio?

Television outstrips radio—and all other media—as the primary source of news, according to the responses of 200 radio and television station managers, 200 news directors, 17 senior broadcasting executives, 21 journalism professors and 600 members of the general public, surveyed by the Radio-Television News Directors Association.[72]

Fifty-four percent of the respondents "claim to depend on television most to obtain news and information," the survey concluded. Another 25 percent cited newspapers as their primary source; but only 14 percent named radio, and a scant 2 percent mentioned magazines.

This should not lead you to ignore radio, however, for its frequency of newscasts and its pervasive daily use by millions of Americans—in automobiles, in the home and on foot—means that it is a useful secondary and reinforcing source of information.

Despite the fact such a small percentage of Americans tell pollsters that they depend on radio for their news, the nation's 4,749 AM and 3,610 FM stations are alive and most are well, with a steady flow of advertising dollars.

The advent of television led to basic changes in radio programming. In the thirties and forties, when radio was a mass entertainment medium, it was what Marshall McLuhan called "cool." That is, your imagination supplied the visual picture to fit the dialogue of the actors in the many dramas, mysteries, soap operas and comedies.

Today, radio is both cool and hot. It is cool in that it supplies endless hours of music of all kinds, conveying virtually no information. It is hot on the news-and-information side, because it conveys a great deal of information in brief but frequent newscasts. Hottest of all are the all-news stations, such as the CBS-owned-and-operated ones in several large cities. These, and others like them, give the network news at the beginning of the hour, followed by regional and local news and a variety of features.

It is this hot side of radio, of course, that should be of interest to you if you are interested in making effective use of every opportunity to talk back.

GETTING ON THE AIR

Many radio stations are extremely profitable for their owners because they are highly automated. Hours of music, interspersed with commercial spots, are taped in advance. The engineer on duty flipping the switches is about as "live" as the station ever gets—except for the news. Local music stations of this type probably have no news staff to cover your news conference or edit your press release. Instead, they will rely on "news feeds" from the Associated Press (AP) or United Press International (UPI), both of which have radio correspondents in most of their bureaus.

If you direct your story or tape to these specialists and they decide to use it, chances are a large number of subscriber stations will end up using it too.

Around the country, 847 stations are members of the Mutual Broadcasting System (MBS), which has a news unit based in Washington, D.C. That is the place to sell your story to Mutual.

Another network that is especially important if you want to reach a well-educated "upscale" audience is National Public Radio (NPR), with 304 member stations. Its "Morning Edition" and "All Things Considered" during afternoon commute time are both edited in NPR's Washington, D.C. headquarters. NPR has a well-regarded news and feature staff at its headquarters and also uses stories from member stations' correspondents. Because NPR is noncommercial (stations are partially supported by listener contributions; the network by grants from businesses, foundations and public subsidies), it has the time to do in-depth features. Stories of eight or nine minutes duration, with several interviews in them, are not uncommon. By contrast, network radio news stories in the five-minute, top-of-the-hour newscasts, are very brief.

News headquarters for the ABC, CBS and NBC radio networks are in New York; however, their owned-and-operated stations (O-and-Os) in major cities have their own news departments and also serve as story sources for the networks. Larger affiliates of the networks have news departments, as do some major independents, such as Los Angeles' all-news KFWB.

If you are called by a radio reporter for an over-the-telephone or in-person interview, follow the same rules you would for a television interview, minus the concern for the camera. Before the interview begins have your communications objective clearly worked out. Plan to give the reporter two or more sound bites of 10 to 20 seconds each.

If you need a moment to phrase an answer to a question, avoid the temptation to buy time by saying "ahh" or "uhh." Remember, the reporter's tape recorder is running, so buy time by keeping your mouth closed. A few seconds of silence will be edited from the interview tape. Your "ahh" or "uhh" may not be.

Opportunites for spontaneous radio interviews often arise from news conferences or briefings. Let us say your company is announcing a new product, plant or policy. You make your statement and answer questions. The event comes to an end, but a radio reporter, with a tape recorder in hand or slung over the shoulder, approaches you for additional comments. This is your opportunity to elaborate on your communications objectives. Remember, radio has an insatiable appetite for news material. They have a lot of time to fill.

ACTUALITIES

Another way to respond to radio's steady demand for material is to make use of "actualities." An actuality is a sort of force-fed sound bite. You record a concise statement (or several), then feed them by telephone to the stations you want to cover.

Radio actualities have several advantages over video clips used as news releases for television stations and cable systems. They can be made quickly; they are inexpensive and easy to disseminate; and they can be made in your office, using nothing more complicated than a portable tape recorder, a set of alligator clips (available at any radio or stereo supply store) and two telephones with a line in common.

If your company or organization dispenses news and features with great regularity, you will want to look into more sophisticated actuality equipment, and perhaps even a soundproofed recording booth—for greater automation and high quality reproduction. For the occasional need, however, the minimal equipment described above will do the job.

Here is how it works. After you have recorded one, two or three brief statements that capsulize the issue, your public relations staff telephones the news rooms of the radio stations you want to reach, describing the content and precise length of each actuality.

First, your staff people will have inserted the male plug end of the alligator clip wires into the tape recorder and attached the two alligator clips to each of the two prongs inside the speaker segment of the telephone receiver (first unscrewing and removing the cover). When a station news director agrees to accept the actualities, your public relations officer simply switches from the extension being used to the one with the alligator-clipped speaker. Then the p. r. person turns on the tape recorder and is transmitting directly to the radio station's recording equipment. On completion, the transmission is verified. The whole operation takes about five minutes per station.

Because of radio's immediacy, actualities may be the only media avenue open to you on short notice, such as at the end of the week. This case illustrates the point.

In 1983 and early 1984, my company had as a client the Committee for Fair Insurance Rates, an insurance coalition opposing federal legislation that would have prohibited insurance companies from using gender as a distinction in setting policy rates. The National Organization for Women (NOW) and other proponents of this so-called Unisex Insurance bill claimed that insurance companies "discriminated" against women, when, in practice, what the insurance companies did was look at their actuarial statistics to see that year after year women lived longer than men (so should pay less for life insurance), had fewer auto accidents than men (so should pay less for auto insurance) and used their health insurance policies more than men (so should pay more for health insurance). The industry projected the costs of passage of the Unisex legislation to its customers and found that, on balance, American women would pay approximately $700 million more a year for insurance. Proponents of the bill conceded that insurance for women might cost more, but argued that "equality" was more important.

On a Tuesday, one week, we learned that on the following Saturday there would be a seminar at Rutgers University in New

Brunswick, New Jersey on women's issues. The insurance issue was to be included on the agenda.

The seminar had been organized by Rep. James Florio (Democrat from New Jersey), who had run for governor in 1981 and appeared to be interested in the job again in 1985. The chairperson of our client coalition, a woman insurance executive, asked Florio's office for an opportunity to address the seminar. The answer was "no," despite the fact that pro-Unisex insurance speakers were scheduled. In addition, several New Jersey state officials were listed on the program and we were concerned that the media might take this as a quasi-endorsement of the positions prevailing at the seminar. Meanwhile, the federal legislation was reaching a critical point in Congress. It was important that our side's point of view be registered so that coverage of the Rutgers seminar did not look as if the pro-Unisex position was unchallenged.

There are no commercial television stations in New Jersey and we did not believe that New York or Philadelphia stations would be greatly interested either in the seminar or in opposing arguments by our client executives. We dispatched press releases to New Jersey's daily newspapers for possible weekend use, but it was radio that got our fullest attention.

On Friday afternoon we offered actualities of the chairwoman of the Committee for Fair Insurance Rates to New Jersey radio stations. She had made two. One covered the point that the Unisex insurance bill would cause economic harm to large numbers of women, especially working women. The other made the point that special interests, for their own reasons, were seeking to have politics rather than the marketplace determine insurance policy rates.

A majority of the stations accepted the actualities over the telephone, and several used them that evening and on Saturday, normally a slow news day.

Actualities can also be used effectively to amplify your original message. Let us say, for example, that your organization is involved in a controversy. The media flock to your office for a "news availability" (informal version of a news conference, called on short notice). They hear your side of the story, but you want to make doubly sure your communications objective gets through the next day. So, after the media leave, you do actualities and offer them to key radio stations. Here is an example of actualities-as-amplifiers from the world of politics:

In the 1976 and 1980 Reagan presidential campaigns, a young man with a tape recorder was assigned to record everything Mr. Reagan said in the presence of media people. This included formal news conferences, news availabilities, one-on-one interviews in autos and airplanes, planeside and curbside exchanges with the media, and so forth. The basic purpose of this effort was to have an accurate record of the candidate's statements in case there was any later dispute over what he had said. Thus, if a reporter came up to one of us and said, "Did you hear him say such-and-such?" we could verify the assertion. We could also bring the matter to the candidate's attention so it would not catch him by surprise if the assertion came up again at his next media encounter.

A secondary benefit of this day-in, day-out tape-recording was that we had good—and ample—material for radio actualities. When the campaign team had settled in for the evening, the man doing the recording would select possible sound bites. We would review them, then pick two or three. He would prepare the actuality tape and a list of stations in the region. Then, early the next morning, local volunteers would come to the hotel to telephone the stations and play the actualities. Thus, hours after the Reagan campaign groups had left town, the candidate's voice was being heard by local radio listeners. In effect, we obtained an extra day's worth of local coverage.

In the hypothetical case of your organization's controversy, a variation on this approach could be used. Make sure your news availability is tape-recorded by your staff. Then, lift two or three actualities from it. Have your staff prepare the edited actuality tape, then call the stations late that day or the next morning.

Chances are, several will use it and you will be more certain of extending your basic message to the audience you want to reach, especially if your actuality is picked up in "drive-time" news, 4-6 P.M. and 7-9 A.M.

6/ Print Media: Newspapers, Newsletters, Magazines

NEWSPAPERS

Newspapers aren't what they used to be. Start with the paperboy. Remember the kid down the street who used to learn thrift, self-discipline and independence by working a paper route, seeing to it that your evening paper was on the doorstep when you got home from work? Well, he isn't there any more. He went on to college and is in business somewhere. His place has been taken by a man in a car who tosses the morning paper on your driveway at 6 A.M.

Today, more Americans get their newspapers in the morning than in the evening, a reversal of the pattern of only a few years ago. Indeed, the evening newspaper is a dying breed, usually combining with its commonly owned morning "sister" to form a single "all-day" paper. This means that home delivery is in the morning, and two or three street editions are turned out, up to mid-afternoon.

What Readers Look For

Not only has there been a basic shift in the organization of the newspaper business—largely as a result of the growth of television—but there has also been a shift in the role newspapers play in our lives.

When television was in its salad days and most newspapers were evening publications, the day's newspaper was often our first source of the day's news. It was a compendium of what had gone on that day (at least up until the early afternoon deadline). Television has long since taken over the role as the principal source of the day's headlines; however, according to a 1984 public opinion survey sponsored by the American Society of Newspaper Editors (ASNE), the newspaper's ability to cover the details of an event has kept the medium from going the way of the dinosaurs.[73]

What the pollsters learned was that readers are looking for hard news—local, regional, state and national. They want factual information—not treatises on how to cope—about such things as health, science, nutrition, child care and technology.

Readers think of newspapers as an indispensable part of their day and something of a bargain. They say that television and computers won't replace their newspaper. However, they also have some doubts about whether newspapers are always fair and unbiased in their coverage and allocation of space.

The pollsters found these conclusions to be strikingly different from those of a similar poll of newspaper readers conducted in 1978 ("Changing Needs of Changing Readers"). They write,

"Then, it was *me, my life, my problems, my environment;* now it is *news, facts, basic information.*"[74]

So, just as television is the ultimate cool medium—highly impressionistic, playing on the emotions and inviting the viewer's imagination to fill in the details—newspaper is seen as the essential dispenser of all the hard facts—the hot medium.

Sketchiness in the Media

A question in the ASNE survey, on the sketchiness of television versus newspaper coverage, bears this out. In the 1978 survey, 53 percent of the respondents said that "TV news is too sketchy—not enough details." Forty-two percent said the same thing of newspapers. In 1984, the gap had widened sharply. Now, 64 percent say that television news is "too sketchy"; but the percentage saying this of newspapers has dropped 12 points, to only 30 percent.

Still, according to this survey, readers retain some skepticism toward the medium. A majority (57%) do not feel that newspaper stories *in general* are fair, yet only 39 percent believe their *own* newspapers are not fair. A parallel exists when it comes to accuracy. Fifty-three percent do not believe that newspapers *in general* are accurate, yet 84 percent described their *own* newspapers as accurate. This tells us that reader loyalty tends to be strong and that it is the other fellow's or the other city's newspaper that is biased and inaccurate.

The implication in this for you as a business executive about to be interviewed by a newspaper reporter is: Don't expect readers to cast much doubt on the veracity of their favorite local newspaper and its writers and editors. You're on your own, more or less.

Sensationalizing the News

Another indication that people take their newspaper more seriously than they do television turns up in the answers to a question in the ASNE survey about "sensationalizing" the news. Those agreeing that television sensationalizes the news "to make it interesting": 81 percent. Those agreeing that newspapers do the same: 52 percent.

That is no sterling mark for newspapers, but compared to television it underscores the survey's conclusion that people rely more on newspapers than television for factual information.

Increased Readership

People are reading their newspapers more often, too, according to the ASNE survey. Young people, especially, are paying more attention to newspapers than they did six years before the 1984 survey. Seventy-four percent of the 18- to 24-year-olds told the pollsters that they read newspapers more frequently. In the 25- to 34-year-old age group, the increased frequency is 57 percent; in the 35-to-49 group, 41 percent; and in the over-50 group, 29 percent.

Respondents told the pollsters they like business news and want more of it. When asked for a list of subjects "that deserve a lot [or at least] some coverage," respondents put business news at the top of the list (83%), followed by consumer news (81%), health, nutrition and medical advice (78%), environmental news (76%) and editorials (74%). Men and women were almost even (80% and 81%, respectively) in saying that business news should be given more space.

The business page editor could be doing a better job, according to the respondents to this survey. Only 67 percent said their most-read newspaper's coverage of "local business briefs" (the only specific business category listed) was "excellent" or "pretty good." This ranking was a tie for 12th place in a list of 22 categories of news coverage.

Inasmuch as U.S. newspaper editors commissioned the survey, we can infer that they will read its results closely and act accordingly. This should mean an increased commitment to business news. It will mean more reporters poking around for stories, but it will also mean a more receptive environment for genuinely interesting stories behind various business successes (and failures) and the men and women who make the companies run.

The opportunities inherent in this deduction carry with them some danger, too. When asked to rate unsatisfactory performance on the part of their most-read newspaper, the ASNE survey respondents gave investigative reporting a 60 percent "unsatisfactory" rating, putting it in third place behind school and education news (64%) and news of Central America

(63%). If those editors read the results as closely as we have surmised, they will be goading their investigative reporters to sharpen their skills. So, if you have a skeleton in the corporate closet you should begin developing your answers to the questions that may come.

How to Be Interviewed

The general rules for being interviewed that were covered in Chapter Three also apply to newspaper interviews, and much of what you read about broadcast interviews in Chapters Four and Five are applicable, minus the requirements for the television camera and radio microphone. There are, however, some important particulars to remember about newspaper interviews:

1. HELP BUILD THE STORY. Anne Ready, the Los Angeles media training consultant, says that the biggest mistake she finds among clients who are print media interview subjects is that they tend to leave it to the reporter "to make the points and sort things out." Thus, only the reporter gives direction to the story. Remedy this by going into the interview with your objective clearly set in advance, then communicate it in your answers or bridge over to it from answers to semi-related subjects.

Compile a list of points you want to make in the interview—your main communications objective, plus supporting points. Study your list well. Commit it to memory, but don't use the material in a wooden, rote manner during the interview. Work it in during the normal flow of conversation.

The reporter is very likely to use your points in the story. Even if he or she goes into the interview, as some do, seeking to verify a thesis, you can use your points to neutralize negative perceptions and force a rethinking of the validity of his or her thesis.

2. AGREE ON THE GROUND RULES. When the story is printed there will be much hair-tearing in your office over misunderstandings about interview ground rules unless you have clearly established them well in advance. Unless you go over these with the reporter beforehand, he or she will assume the

interview is to be entirely on the record. It is best to agree on the ground rules at the time the reporter first calls to make the appointment. Immediately thereafter, draft a memo for your files about your understanding of the ground rules. Then, when the reporter arrives, review the memo to make sure both of you have the same understanding of them.

Ground rules for interviews probably have the most complex gradations and nuances in Washington, D.C., where at almost any given moment scores of officials are trying to affect various public policies without being identified. They have devised ways of leaking information without their names being used. For the purposes of most business or general interviews, however, there are a few basic rules to choose from:

- *On the record.* It is simple and straightforward. Everything you say in the interview may be quoted. You may—before the interview begins—state a caveat along these lines: "This is on the record; however, if I find that you come to a question where my answer must be 'off the record' or 'not for attribution,' I will so state." If you use this caveat, make a note of any use to which you put it during the interview so that you can commit it to your files afterward.
- *On background.* This means not for attribution specifically to you. Usually, reporters will use the information they get from you without any quotes, since they cannot attribute them. They will find other ways to attribute the information—such as to "company sources," "sources close to the matter," or simply, "our sources."
- *On deep background* usually means that you are requiring reporters to use even more obscure, indirect sourcing. This is frustrating to them, as in "on deep, deep background," which means that not the slightest hint of attribution can be used, so that the reporter themselves appear to be the authorities for the information. This renders the information virtually useless to them. As a general rule, avoid these two restrictive variations of "on background."

* *Off the record.* Use this sparingly, for it means that the reporter may not quote you, attribute the information to you or use the information in any direct sense in a story that would link it to you. Information gleaned off the record may serve to make the reporter better informed in developing the story and it may therefore also serve your purposes under the circumstances, but all of this must be clearly understood by both parties before the interview begins.

When to Talk

While being straightforward with the news media is the best policy most of the time, there are times when you must use caution. For example, if a reporter whose name is unfamiliar to you calls and wants to "ask a few questions," be careful. If your company has reason to believe it may be the target of a hatchet job by some publication—or even if it does not—make sure the reporter identifies his or her publication to your satisfaction. If the reporter is a free-lance writer, ask for the name of the editor for whom this assignment is being done. Make a tentative appointment for an interview, but do not succumb to the pressure tactic of "I'm on deadline." Then check credentials. You can always cancel the interview if they are not satisfactory.

A favorite trick of some free-lance "investigative" reporters is to call their subjects on the pretext of writing a book. Somehow, in the mind of the subject, a book, being long range, reflective and history-oriented, does not seem to pose the danger that a hard-hitting, negative story in next Sunday's *Daily Bugle* would. So, you find yourself giving long, helpful answers to the questions, only to find the reporter's real objective was to sell a newspaper or the wire services a hot investigative story.

I learned a lesson the hard way. Once, during the years between Ronald Reagan's California governorship and the presidency, when Michael Deaver and I coordinated his business activities and were his spokesmen, a young man, whom I took to be a college newspaper writer, called for an interview. Always wanting to cultivate good relations for Reagan with young people,

I granted the interview. I found later that the young man was from one of Ralph Nader's fronts and had intended all along to do a hatchet job on Reagan in a Nader book. By that time, Nader had become somewhat irrelevant on the American scene, so there was no real damage done, but I made a mental note always to check credentials carefully in cases where I did not already know the reporter.

When you are interviewed you do not have to answer every question, nor do you have to be defensive about not answering some. For example, if your company's stock is not publicly traded, you are not required to release financial data if you want it to remain confidential. Some reporters use intimidation; most learn to ask the same question six or seven ways in order to extract the information they want. In either case, if you do not want to give the information and it is not already a matter of public record, you can politely decline to answer. (Example: During those same years with private citizen Ronald Reagan, we were often asked by reporters for the amount of his fee for giving a speech to a business group. We would reply by saying that we were sorry, but that our policy was not to discuss these arrangements since they were private. This answer was always accepted at face value. In fact, many reporters had correctly guessed the amount of Reagan's fees, but we would never confirm or deny their guesses.)

Don't repeat a reporter's questions. Sometimes the questions will be benign, but often they will be intended to lead you. If, for example, the interviewer says, "Is your plan to move the Centerville plant still causing you trouble?", your answer should not be, "No, the relocation is not causing us any trouble." That not only sounds defensive, but it also gives the reporter a quote from you that reinforces the negative suspicion that the plant relocation is indeed causing you fits. Instead, your answer should be along the lines of, "We want everyone involved to understand why it is essential that we move this plant and how it can be done without a negative impact on our work force. We have been making real progress in getting our program understood." In other words, accentuate the positive and, in the words of that World War II song, "eliminate the negative."

Putting your best foot forward in a newspaper interview is always important. Whether the interview is *on the record* or *on background*, give clear, concise, truthful answers to the reporter's questions. This will serve the interests of all concerned.

The opposite approach sours the atmosphere for good business-media relations. I recall this statement by the public relations director of a large bank at a recent conference: "The *Wall Street Journal* [news pages] may seem to have an anti-business bias, but if you had been lied to by as many business people as most *Journal* reporters probably have, you would be skeptical about business, too."

NEWSLETTERS

Most of the interview rules that apply to newspapers apply to newsletters as well, but remember that newsletters, by their very nature, are in the business of spotting trends and passing on gossip about the field they are covering. They use relatively few direct quotes, relying more on "inside" background information. Thus, in giving a newsletter editor an on-background interview, you may want to be more cautious than you would be with a newspaper reporter, because the narrow range of the newsletter's circulation may make it easier for readers to identify you or your organization as the source of a particular item or story.

MAGAZINES

Here, again, most of the same interview rules apply. Magazines, however, because of their usually long lead times (up to 90 days in the case of some monthlies), require that you answer your interviewer's questions with the future clearly in mind. You must think ahead to when the interview will be published. Frame your answers in the context of what you think will be correct and timely then, rather than the present. For example, if the annual trade show will have been held between now and then, don't talk about it in the future tense. Or if an important industry statistic not now known will be released by then, you will have to work around it if it comes up for discussion in an interview held today.

Having covered the major media, broadcast and print, we move now to a variety of media encounters you may find yourself involved in, voluntarily or otherwise.

7/ A Variety of Media Encounters

NEWS CONFERENCES, AVAILABILITIES, BRIEFINGS

If a negative story breaks about your company or organization, someone will inevitably want to talk back to the media by way of a news conference. It will seem like a quick, dramatic way to "set the record straight." Be careful, though. Like an angry letter, the idea is best left to cool off awhile, then reconsidered.

The greatest danger in holding a news conference in the wake of unfavorable reportage is that you will make what might otherwise be a one-day story into a two-day (or more) story. Furthermore, you and your colleagues may be overreacting to the initial story. Remember, very few people will care as much about a story as the subjects of the story, whose pride and self-esteem may have been temporarily wounded. Human nature is to think that the whole world is paying as much attention as we are to stories about things we care about. But it ain't necessarily so. In fact, it is rarely so.

Before calling a news conference to rebut a negative story, assess the actual and potential damage from the negative assertions or "tone" of the story. If they seem considerable, plan your news conference opening statement carefully and review with your key colleagues possible questions you will be asked.

Remember, holding a news conference tells the media that you take the initial negative story very seriously. If you want to respond in a lower-voltage way, consider a "news availability." This is informal in tone, held in your office conference room and called on relatively short notice. The company's spokesperson may be seated, to convey the feeling that the organization is responding in a calm, measured way to the bad news. He or she will give a brief opening statement, then answer questions. The amount of time devoted to the news availability is usually less than that for a formal news conference, but not by much. A news conference will typically run 20 minutes. (An associate of the spokesperson should stand by, watching for signs of reporters closing their notebooks and putting pens and pencils away. That is the time to say, "time for one more question.") An availability should have a we've-got-to-get-back-to-work quality to it when you are responding to a negative story, so it may conclude after 10 to 15 minutes.

If, on sober reflection about the negative story, you still believe that a full-scale news conference is the best way to respond, give thought to the time and place. If you want to be on the evening news, a mid-morning news conference is best, beginning at 10:00 or 10:30 A.M. This also suits most newspapers, for reporters write their stories for tomorrow the afternoon before.

Do not build news conferences around meals such as breakfast or lunch (for news *briefings* that is another matter, as we shall see). For news conferences, the media people expect news and they want to get it straight and in as little time as necessary. If you hold a mid-morning news conference in, say, a meeting room of a conveniently located hotel (avoid clubs except the press club because of elitist or all-male imagery), have a table in the back of the room with coffee, orange juice, ice water and Danish pastries. Set the chairs as if for a lecture, with an opening in the center (facing those who will speak) for a low-rise platform for television cameras (these are standard items at most hotels). Speak from a lectern and, if possible, obtain from a communications supply dealer a "mult" box that permits many microphones to be plugged into it and your spokesperson to speak from only one. Thus, the unsightly pile of microphones taped to the lectern, with spaghetti-like chords draped from them, won't be around to distract viewers.

Whether it is a formal news conference or an informal news availability, make a brief opening statement that conveys your organization's objective. Have copies handed out as reporters arrive so they can study them and frame their questions.

Another time many companies think of calling a news conference is when there is good news to tell, such as the introduction of a new product or service. Even if you are certain that the news is worth more than just a press release, if it is not stop-the-press news, consider an alternative to a news conference, a news briefing. If companies and other organizations call news conferences at the drop of a hat and the events turn out to be thin in terms of hard news, the media feel cheated and become reluctant to answer the next news conference call.

A news media briefing (a better term than "press briefing," since broadcast media people think "press" means only newspapers and magazines) is informal, relaxed and nonconfrontational. Breakfast or lunch are good settings for news briefings. Again, a hotel meeting room is the best location. A cocktail party is less desirable because your audience will be paying less attention; however, this format is sometimes used for new product introductions.

Briefings done at meals usually span a one-and-a-half-hour period. When inviting the media, make it clear the event will conclude on time. Remember, some of the reporters may want to write about it the same day. A few may want to linger for individual interviews with the spokesperson after the event concludes.

In all three cases—news conferences, availabilities and briefings—mail or deliver a media advisory memo giving purpose, time, date, place (the availability, because it is often called on short notice, may have to be called in entirely by phone). Follow-through telephone calls to each person on the invitation list should be made the day before the event. The wire service "day books" should be notified, and you should consider using one of the business wire services, such as PR Newswire. The rest of the list will depend on the nature of your organization and the topic to be covered.

CONGRESSIONAL HEARINGS

Congressional hearings, as often as not, are conceived and called for the purpose of getting attention from the news media for a particular point of view about a particular subject. Whatever you have learned from your experience or this book that helps you improve your handling of interviews, news conferences, availabilities and briefings will also be helpful it you find yourself testifying at a Congressional hearing. There are also some special things to remember.

If you are called to testify at a hearing, you will find yourself in one of two roles: *expert witness* or *villain*. When you are first called by a Congressional commitee investigator or other staff member, it may not be obvious which role the hearing's organizers have in mind for you. You need to find out. If you can't ascertain it from your first contact, analyze a list of the members of the committee or subcommittee calling the hearing. Either the chairperson will have called it on his or her own volition or at the request of members of the committee's or subcommittee's majority. Thus, with a little research you can deduce whether the hearing will be neutral—that is, whether it will really be seeking information—or will be Congressional Theater, intended to reinforce the existing position of the chairman and majority or to attempt to score some points with the voters back home by looking for scapegoats in a current issue.

If you have determined that you are being asked to testify as an expert witness because of your credentials within your industry or profession, you can relax in the knowledge that most of the questions will be friendly. If you know the objectives of those who called the hearing and you are in agreement with them, it will be all the easier.

Whether you are being asked to testify as an expert witness—an essentially neutral role—or "villain" (that is, to defend your company or industry), find out if you can make an opening statement. If so, ascertain how long it should be. This statement should summarize your knowledge of the issue and your position on it. Find out how many copies the committee wants for distribution and have them prepared. If you are an expert witness, it does not matter how far in advance you deliver the copies of your testimony. If, on the other hand, you think you are going to be cast as a villain, deliver the advance copies as close to the time of your actual appearance as possible. This is to prevent committee staff members from giving your inquisitors time to digest your material.

Ambitious Congressional staff members are often the driving force behind the investigations that lead to hearings. They want to make their employers—the committee chairperson and majority members—look good, and they want to look good themselves. Veterans at this business on Capitol Hill are usually very good at it. One of the best known, Frank Silbey, left the Hill (Senate Judiciary Committee; House Government Operations) in March 1984 to open his own counseling firm. According to his announcement release, the firm would offer counsel "to the private sector on actual and/or pending Congressional and other federal inquiries. Once a potential problem arises, PCC [the Silbey firm] can advise top management as to the exact nature of the inquiry."

Many hearings have their genesis in an investigation that is followed by a leak to the press. Tom Bethell, writing in the Spring 1984 issue of *Chief Executive* magazine, says of Silbey, for example, "For years [he] was the Congressional investigator behind some of the most publicized Capitol Hill inquiries...taking leaked documents from disgruntled federal employees, calling up his favorite reporters, handing them scoops on a plate, and persuading the committee chairman to hold public hearings with the promise that he will be regarded as the stout defender of the public interest."

If you are on the business end of such a process, Silbey advises cooperation with the investigators. You should also have legal and public relations counsel from people who know how the Congressional hearing process works.

In his interview with Bethell, Silbey predicted a new surge in Congressional oversight investigations. Such surges often coincide with the convening of a new Congress, which happens at the beginning of every odd-numbered year. Silbey contends that military procurement, chemicals, drugs and nuclear energy will all be likely investigatory and hearing targets for the next several years.

If you have determined that you are being asked to testify in order for some committee members to make your company or industry appear to be a "villain" in a particular issue, there are several things to remember about the way you handle both your prepared testimony and the question-and-answer period:

1. Identify the single most important objective you want to communicate, and develop a concise statement about it. Keep coming back to it during the course of your hearing appearance.
2. Treat all questioners seriously and politely.
3. Do not lose your temper.

4. You will be sitting at a table. Sit up straight and avoid distracting gestures or mannerisms.
5. Assume that every moment you are in the hearing room will be on the evening TV news. It won't. Perhaps only 20 seconds of it will, but you won't know which 20 seconds.
6. Remember that your questioners will know far less than you do about your subject—if anything. Use the opportunity to educate them without being overlong in your answers or patronizing or pedantic. Talk to them as if you think they know the subject, but discuss it in a way that fills them in on important background details. One good way to impart new knowledge is to say, "As you know…" followed by the information you are fairly sure they do not know.
7. Some of your Congressional questioners will appear to be asking questions from slips of paper fed to them by aides crouching behind them. Do not let this distract you. It is a common practice. While some members of Congress are more conscientious than others about learning the subjects with which they must deal, the use of aides-mémoires from staff members does not necessarily mean that the member is either lazy or uninformed about the matter at hand. Do not draw such conclusions. Rather, proceed in a sincere and straightforward manner.
8. Be prepared for a tussle between your lawyers and your public relations/public affairs people over your written testimony. Lawyers, indispensable though they are, tend to write testimony that is turgid and plodding. Let them develop the first draft, then let your communications experts tighten and polish it.

STAKEOUTS AND HOW TO HANDLE THEM

If testifying at a Congressional hearing doesn't sound like much fun, it will seem like a carefree lark compared to a stakeout. The stakeout is a product of the television age. While radio reporters, print media writers and photographers may all take part in a stakeout, it exists largely to show the quarry cornered on the evening or morning TV news.

Stakeouts are most often employed when high government officials become embroiled in controversy and their continuation in office is problematical. This produces a story of several days (or even weeks) duration. Since it is never quite certain when the story will change in nature (a resignation, announcement of an investigation, exoneration), assignment editors try to cover all bases with reporters and cameras. A residential stakeout is assigned when the issue is thought to be reaching a crisis and, thus, an impending resolution.

Residential stakeouts almost never produce hard news or newsbreaks (although office stakeouts do, because that is where officials would customarily announce their position on a matter or respond to changing events or new charges). Since residential stakeouts, however, are a product of journalism's herd instinct, they are certain to always be with us. Assignment editors may feel nearly sure that a stakeout will be unproductive, but the fear that their station or network may be scooped by the competition impells them to assign a crew to the home of the person at the center of the story.

Your chances of being the subject of a stakeout may seem remote; however, it helps to know how to deal with one in case it should happen to you or an associate.

Stakeouts, especially those of short duration, may be used when a business executive becomes embroiled in a controversy. For example, if you or your organization are defendants in a juicy white-collar crime trial, the media may stake out your home and your office, in the hope of getting a colorful offhand comment from you.

Or, if there is a potential disaster involving your nuclear plant or chemical storage facility, your office may be staked out because that is the place from which news of developments in the matter will emanate.

It is the residential stakeout, however, that is most troublesome because it can become an assault on the privacy of you and your family during a time when you and they will already be under great stress.

Richard V. Allen describes vividly the ordeal of a residential stakeout. He resigned as President Reagan's national security adviser in early January 1982, after he had been cleared of allegations that he had improperly accepted money and gifts from Japanese journalists and business men.

About the stakeout he said:

> We were held captive in our house by the media from roughly mid-November to early January. This was all day, every day. Thanksgiving, Christmas, New Years, weddings, anniversaries, birthdays. They would begin to come at about 5:30 in the morning. I would be forced to respond at 6:30 A.M. upon leaving the house. When I had nothing to say, they tried other ways to get a story. A CBS reporter tried to question my six-year-old daughter on her way to kindergarten. "Is your daddy home?" My kids were afraid to go out.

Allen concludes that "...the process feeds on itself. The *Washington Post* would run a story outlining new and anonymous innuendos directed against me and the network news directors would all feel driven by competitive pressure to try to get a response. The remedy is self-restraint."[75]

The get-the-story imperative, the fear of missing a new development and apprehension over losing out to the competition will inevitably crowd out an assignment editor's interest in self-restraint. Thus, you should have some standby stratagems in mind in the event you or a colleague ever become subject to a stakeout. Here are four:

1. When you leave for work in the morning you will have to face the media gathered in front of your home as Allen did. Smile as you say, "I have nothing to add." Be neither flippant nor carefree, just calm and cheerful (even though you won't feel that way).

2. If the stakeout crews make a mess of your lawn with food and beverage containers and other trash, ask them politely to remove it and to stay off your lawn. If the problem persists, have your lawyer call the editors or managers of the offending media. Trespassing is still illegal.

3. To keep them from being harrassed, move your family temporarily to the home of relatives or friends in another neighborhood. It will give them some needed peace of mind even though you will be separated.

4. Even stakeout crews have to sleep, so, if you can get by on little sleep yourself, come home at midnight and leave for the office at 5:00 A.M. The chances of encountering them will be greatly reduced.

As noted before, if there is a stakeout at your office over a disaster, impending disaster or other major case involving your organization, the rules are different. If you are the CEO and there are reasons why you should not be the principal spokesperson, appoint one from among your colleagues. Instruct him or her to be accessible to the media. If there is a need to have more than one spokesperson (as, for example in the case of an around-the-clock crisis such as a nuclear plant accident), make sure each one has the same information to give the media so confusion is avoided.

We move now from what have been largely defensive situations to talking back to the media in a more aggressive way. Some of the approaches in the next chapter are "low voltage" and one is very high. All of them will have you on the offensive.

8/ Action:
From Letters
to Lawsuits

You open the morning paper; it's there.

Or you flick on the evening news; it's there.

Or you turn on the car radio on the way home; it's there.

It, in each case, is a story that, as you see it, maligns you and/or your organization, impugns your honesty and reputation, and contains specific errors of fact.

Remember the herd instinct discussed in earlier chapters? It will be at work in this case, too. The other media pick up the story and repeat it all over town (or all over the country, depending on the scope of your activities).

You are angry; so angry that your first instinct is to talk back—strike back—immediately.

In this case, your first instinct will be your worst instinct. Your judgment will improve. Meanwhile, the first thing to do in such a situation is *nothing*. You will need time to cool down. A few hours or overnight should do it. You will need to talk about it with your colleagues, your public relations counselor and your lawyer. By then, you will be calmer and your view of the situation much clearer than it was when the story first hit you.

Yes, the story may have been unfair; and in this chapter we shall show how corrective action can turn such situations around. Chances are, however, that the negative story is a result not of a plan to do a "hatchet job," but of a combination of factors such as a different perspective on the part of the reporter and editor; deadline pressures that make full research difficult; background stories from the medium's morgue that contain factual errors; even unwillingness by you or your colleagues to answer reporters' questions, leaving them to draw their own conclusions (probably negative).

After a negative story appears, when you have let the situation cool, there are several types of responses for you to consider. They are listed here in order of increasing intensity and visibility:

1. No response.
2. A letter to the writer of the story.
3. A letter to the editor, not for publication.
4. A letter to the editor, for publication.
5. A counterinterview with another journalist.
6. A formal demand for published correction.
7. A "preemptive reaction" strike.
8. A lawsuit.

At least two of these responses, numbers five and eight, carry the risk of backfiring. At least one, number eight, almost certainly will cost you a good deal of money in lawyer's fees. The rest of this chapter will examine each of these strategies in turn.

NO RESPONSE

The morning after the negative story has appeared, reread it carefully. Or, if it is a television or radio story, review a tape and a transcript. Chances are you will still smart at what you think are wrong and unfair conclusions. Set aside any dark thoughts you have about the motives of the writer and editor for a moment, however, and judge each element of the story in detail. Was the error really an error, a misstatement of fact, or was it, instead, a statement that might lead people to a conclusion you wish they would not make? Remember, you are in possession of far more details about your business or profession than either the reporter or the audience. Ask yourself, also, how much the seemingly erroneous statement actually matters to the health of your business. Yes, it may have been poorly researched, and it may have been sloppily written. And, yes, the reporter may have some antibusiness prejudice or even the arrogance of an ambitious hotshot out to make a mark. But does the story really damage you and your organization? And, ask yourself, is it a one-day story? If it is, then write an angry letter to the editor, put it in your desk for 24 hours, then read it again before you drop it in the wastebasket.

In doing research for this chapter, I talked with several veteran reporters about the matter of an instant hot retort to a negative story. They all shared the view just expressed. They acknowledged that mistakes are made, that sometimes a story is slanted and that there are steps to take in such cases, but that more often than not the story that gets us hot under the collar is not worth a response.

WRITING TO THE WRITER OF THE STORY

If the story does contain factual errors and you want to make sure the record is corrected without getting into a protracted argument (or inviting a second story), consider writing a letter directly to the writer of the story (or on-the-air correspondent if it is a broadcast story). Good reporters pride themselves on accuracy, and this private correction will usually be appreciated (though it may not be acknowledged). The reporter will undoubtedly be much more careful if he or she is assigned to do another story on you; however, this private, for-the-files, not-for-publication approach to factual errors will not protect you in the event another reporter is assigned to do a story on you at a later date. That reporter will go to the morgue or filed tapes on you and on the earlier story, and will treat the earlier story as correct, in the absence of any note in the file to the effect that this or that fact had been challenged. So, the letter to the writer of the story can be useful, but it is limited in value.

A LETTER TO THE EDITOR, NOT FOR PUBLICATION

This letter escalates the private letter to the writer by a degree. It tells the editor you are not trying to embarrass the publication by seeking to rebut a story in print, but it also announces that you take the story seriously and want to make sure that future accuracy is assured. Such a letter should note that its purpose is not publication but to make sure that future references to you and/or your organization do not carry erroneous information. Ask the editor to give a copy of the letter to the writer of the story, if it is bylined, or to the publication's ombudsman if it has one. The writer, especially if a young one, may not like this, but it should have the desired effect of making this particular news organization more careful in the future.

...AND FOR PUBLICATION

Letters to the editor for publication fall into two categories: (1) correction of errors; and (2) rebuttal of arguments.

The first usage falls under the heading of "damage control." Let us assume that a negative story with factual errors has been printed or broadcast about you or your organization. You fear negative consequences in any of several forms: reaction of customers and suppliers; damaged employee morale; reduced shareholder confidence.

One of the demands of news reporting—simplification of complicated subjects—is working against you when you sit down to compose a letter to the editor that you hope will be published. You will feel the urge to rebut each error or misleading statement categorically and in detail. Indeed, for clarity, you will almost certainly have to lead the reader through a complicated explanation of the subject in order to get him or her to understand that the reporter's oversimplification resulted in an incorrect conclusion or impression.

Forget it.

Instead, select only two or three of the most egregious errors or oversimplifications. Cite them to reestablish the context, and correct them as economically as you can in order to keep the letter under 200 words. If there are more errors than these, you can make an opening note in your letter to the effect that such-and-such story "contained a number of errors, the most serious of which are these: ...."

Respond to the story promptly, after allowing for the cooling-off period mentioned earlier. If you are going to send a letter, do it the day following the story, after you have thought about it and conferred with your advisers. If you decide to send the letter, telephone the person in charge of letters to the editor at the publication (broadcast stations do not have such an outlet). Alert him or her that the letter is coming. Chances are, the news organization will pay close attention to it. The editor's sense of fair play will be activated. Alerting the medium is important because there are always more letters than there is space to print them; a letter from one who has been the subject of a current story will almost certainly be given priority.

Send the letter by one of the overnight courier services or priority mail so that it is sure to reach its destination the following day. Send it to the attention of the person to whom you talked.

The second type of letter to the editor, for publication, is not intended for damage control but to seize an opportunity to extend the argument for a particular side of an issue. In this case, the letter is sent not as often in response to a news story as it is in reply to an editorial or op-ed page article about the subject.

The same rules about length and promptness apply, although there is no need to alert the person in charge of letters to the editor that your letter is on the way.

A COUNTER INTERVIEW

Returning to the negative story about you or your organization, let us say that on reflection you have decided to counterattack, literally to talk back to the medium that published or broadcast a harmful story. One stratagem for doing this is to find a journalist who may be sympathetic to your position in the matter or whose instincts for fair play have been aroused by what he or she sees as unfair treatment by a competing medium.

If you find such a journalist under the particular circumstances, remember the risk you are taking: You have no control over the resulting story and, unless you are willing to be very straightforward in the counterinterview and have strong supporting evidence that the negative story was seriously in error, slanted, or both, you may find that the counterinterview only makes things worse.

No journalist wants to be manipulated, and even one who feels you may have been wronged by another medium is going to look for fresh information, rather than a recitation of self-justifying statements from you or your colleagues.

DEMANDING A PUBLISHED CORRECTION

Consult both your public relations and legal counsel before taking this step. To demand published correction or retraction of a reference to you or your organization when the reference is simply one with which you are uncomfortable is to invite a flat turndown from the medium.

If the story contained a specific error of fact, which might give an incorrect impression that is unfavorable to you, then ask for a correction. Some newspapers run correction columns or boxes on the same page, day in and day out (the *Washington Post* runs one daily on p. 2). The content of these, however, is usually limited to corrections of typographical errors or other minor mistakes that, inadvertently, may have created a wrong impression.

Mistaken identity is a legitimate reason for demanding a correction, particularly if the potentially injured party is a public figure or otherwise well known.

On September 5, 1984 the *Los Angeles Times* ran a boxed correction on p. 3 that pointed out that a June 30th story had reported that a Malibu, California landowner had managed to persuade the state legislature to come up with $9 million to buy his 275 acres of brushland for a park. The earlier story also noted that state park officials the year before had said they did not want the property, and federal officials had estimated its worth at $1.7 million.

The newspaper went on to say, "the *Times* incorrectly identified the landowner as former state Public Utilities Commissioner Leonard M. Ross. The *Times* confused one Leonard M. Ross with another Leonard M. Ross."

The article went on to detail the circumstances and to include a photograph of the former state official who had been incorrectly identified in the story.

The *Times* noted that it had published a page-one correction of the error the day after it had occurred; but apparently Leonard M. Ross, the former state official, continued to get embarrassing questions about his alleged involvement in the matter so he had his lawyers contact the *Times* for an expanded correction in order that there would be no doubt that he was not the Leonard M. Ross who had been accused of lobbying the state legislature.

At the conclusion of its two-column-wide, right-inch-deep second correction box, the *Times* admitted that its reporters had not attempted to reach Ross, the former official. It said the reporters had made several attempts to reach the landowner, with no success. Apparently, making no contact, they drew the conclusion the Rosses were one and the same.

If your lawyer writes a letter to a medium demanding a correction, that medium will take it seriously because the act of writing such a letter implies legal action if they do not. Thus, your lawyer will not counsel in favor of such an approach unless your case is a strong one. In Ross' case he was an innocent party, potentially injured. The facts were on his side and the case clear. Thus, he finally got the *mea culpa* he wanted from the newspaper.

PREEMPTIVE REACTION STRIKES

This strategy, with its military terminology, is one to use when negative media references to you have become virtually epidemic as a result of some earlier controversy. If the facts are on your side, the technique can be very effective; however, you will still need to consult your lawyer before you use it.

Consider the case of Richard V. Allen, President Reagan's national security adviser from the beginning of his first term in January 1981 until early January 1982.

In November 1981, Allen became the center of a controversy when $1,000 was found in his office safe. He had intercepted the money from two Japanese women journalists on the first day of the Reagan term when they met first lady Nancy Reagan for a brief interview. They had intended to proffer the money (which was in an envelope) as an honorarium for the interview, a not uncommon custom on the part of Japanese interviewers.

Allen gave the envelope to his secretary to put in the safe that evening so that it could be turned over to the proper authorities the next day for disposal. In the rush of business, however, the envelope was forgotten, not turning up till months later when new occupants of the office in which the safe was located happened upon it.

The context in which all this occurred included the fact that Allen and then Secretary of State Alexander Haig were frequently at swords' points and each had his supporters and detractors. One of Allen's detractors leaked the information about the $1,000 find to the media, and the herd came running.

Up to this time, Ronald Reagan's presidency had been gaining policy victory after policy victory, seemingly impervious to criticism. This situation frustrated many in the media in Washington, and the Allen revelation provided the "red meat" some of them had been seeking.

Despite solemn protestations by editors at civic luncheons about "objectivity" and dedication to "fairness," the fact is that when a controversy reaches critical mass in the media—especially if it involves official Washington—the central figure in the controversy is treated by the media as being guilty until proven innocent. Such was the atmosphere surrounding the Allen case for the six weeks from mid-November until Allen resigned in early January 1982.

Thorough investigations of Allen's actions were conducted by both the U.S. Department of Justice and the White House counsel's office. He was cleared in both instances.

On January 4, 1982 Allen resigned, not as a result of the investigations, but because of internal White House politics and policy differences. He returned to private life as an international trade consultant, which he remains to this day.

Ever since his resignation, however, Allen has found that almost any time he has been mentioned in the media the original allegations stick to him like tar. Example: A biographical box preceding an interview with Allen on national security in *USA Today* began, "Richard Allen, 47, resigned as National Security

Adviser for President Reagan following allegations that he accepted bribes from Japanese journalists."[76]

In this and other instances, Allen talked back—and fast. The next day, the newspaper ran a boxed amplification and correction, and Allen received a letter of apology from editorial director John Siegenthaler.

Allen soon found himself repeating this sequence of events with such frequency that he decided on a much broader strategy, the "preemptive reaction" strike, with the intention of preventing such loosely researched and negative references in the future.

Allen conferred with his attorney at the major Washington firm of Arnold & Porter. They agreed upon a strategy that would involve sending a letter with a thick enclosure to approximately 100 columnists, commentators and news organizations throughout the country. The enclosure, which had eight sections and ran to 56 pages, is described in attorney William D. Rogers' cover letter that was mailed on September 10, 1984. The letter reads as follows:

> We are writing to you on behalf of our client, Richard V. Allen. Mr. Allen was formerly assistant to the President for National Security Affairs; he resigned on January 4, 1982, and is now a private consultant in Washington, D.C.
>
> Mr. Allen, an acknowledged expert in the fields of international affairs, national security affairs and international and economic trade policy, is frequently the subject of news stories and interviews on substantive issues. In this connection, media accounts sometimes appear purporting to describe the events prior to and surrounding his resignation from government.
>
> One such account appeared in the April 5, 1983 issue of *USA Today*, a copy of which may be found at Tab A of the enclosure. The prologue to this article contained serious errors and was highly misleading. It failed to state that there were in fact no formal allegations against Mr. Allen; that Mr. Allen was completely cleared of any wrongdoing after a thorough investigation by the Department of Justice and the office of the Counsel to the President. It also implied that Mr. Allen

resigned from office as a result of these rumors and innuendos, when in fact his resignation resulted solely from differences of a policy or political nature within the Administration.

In response to a strong representation by Mr. Allen, *USA Today* published an apology and retraction on April 6, and in a letter from John Siegenthaler, Editorial Director, tendered its regrets and apologies to Mr. Allen. Copies of the article, retraction and the letter of apology from the Editorial Director of *USA Today* will also be found at Tab A of the attachment to this letter.

The attorney's letter goes on to recount similar instances of incorrect references followed by retractions, corrections and/or letters of apology from the *Wall Street Journal*, syndicated columnists Joseph Kraft and James J. Kilpatrick, *New York Times* columnist Anthony Lewis and ABC's "World News Tonight."

The letter concludes with a roundhouse punch:

> ...we feel compelled to put you on notice that any incorrect, incomplete or misleading reference to Mr. Allen, including direct or implied statements that he accepted bribes or unlawful gifts while in office or conducted himself in an unethical manner; accepted payment in connection with an interview with the First Lady; the failure to mention Mr. Allen's exoneration by the Justice Department and the Counsel to the President following exhaustive and detailed investigations; and any innaccurate description of the circumstances surrounding his resignation as Assistant to the President, will be actionable at law.

Did this carefully detailed letter, with its strongly worded ending, work? Did it meet Allen's objective to stop the nearly automatic negative references to him whenever his name was mentioned in the media? So far, it has been a complete success, according to Allen. Not only have no new negative references been published or broadcast, but the act of sending the letter and packet of materials has generated a good deal of media attention. *Fortune*, on October 15, 1984, wrote a two-column story about Allen's stratagem under the headline, "PREEMPTIVE

STRIKE—Richard Allen warns the press not to spread misinformation about how he left government."

Not only did this salvo achieve its purpose, but so did each of the individual demands for published or broadcast corrections that led up to it. Note that in each case where there were errors of fact, Allen moved quickly to demand corrections and apologies. By the time he had six such cases on file, he conferred with his attorneys and decided on the strategy to circulate widely a detailed warning that he took his honor seriously enough to sue any news organization that treated it casually.

Back during the height of the Allen controversy in late 1981, he employed another unorthodox strategy. Hounded daily by the media and suspicious that television news editors would edit any interviews in a way that would portray him negatively, he avoided all but cursory contact with TV until mid-December. Then, he decided to "go public" with his side. He did not engage legal counsel at the time, although several of his friends urged him to do so. Instead, he approached the media himself, offering to be interviewed, but insisting that in television interviews he appear live on camera. Such a stratagem is worth considering if you or your organization are under serious media fire and you are concerned, as Allen was, that editing might slant an interview against you.

LAW SUITS

The Hugel Case

Max Hugel was as determined as Richard Allen to clear his name, but it took a lawsuit to do it. Hugel, a New Hampshire businessman who had been active in the 1980 Reagan presidential campaign, was named by Central Intelligence Agency director William Casey to be his deputy for operations (including clandestine operations) in May 1981.

Hugel's appointment was not popular with some old CIA hands and other professionals, and stories complaining about

Hugel's lack of experience in the field were generated in the media. Taken by itself, this sort of reaction is not surprising in Washington as a new administration settles in. What changed this brushfire into a conflagration of negative publicity for Max Hugel—publicity that led to his resignation—were two erstwhile securities brokers, Samuel and Thomas McNell, who contacted the *Washington Post* on May 25.

Hugel's background was this: After World War II he had founded an export company in Japan, which later evolved into Brother International, a company that imported and distributed consumer goods in the United States. Brother International went public in 1973, and that year the McNell Securities firm was appointed by Brother to be the principal market maker for its stock. McNell remained so until August 1974 when the McNells ran into trouble—unrelated to Brother—with the Securities and Exchange Commission.

The McNell brothers gave the *Post* tapes purporting to be of their telephone conversations with Hugel in 1974. In these conversations, they alleged, Hugel had given them inside information about his company's financial performance prior to its public disclosure, presumably for the purpose of inflating the value of its stock. (A review of the transcripts of the taped conversations reveals that they were devoted largely to efforts by Hugel to collect some $377,000 lent to Sam McNell who, in turn, had apparently lent it to his brother for the latter's financially ailing securities firm.) The McNells also claimed that Hugel had engaged in other irregular and illegal practices, such as conspiring with the chief executive of another company for him to buy blocks of Brother stock from several brokers to create the impression that the stock was gaining popularity, thus justifying a higher price on the market.

Confronted with the McNells' allegations and the *Post's* possession of their secret tapes, Hugel and his lawyers met with *Post* editors and reporters on Friday, July 10. From the transcript of this meeting, one learns that Hugel and his lawyers requested time to obtain records from Brother International (which he had left in 1975) to buttress Hugel's denial of the allegations. The *Post* executives made a show of reasonableness, but it is clear from the transcript that they were anxious to get the story and get it first. The parties agreed to talk again on Monday, July 13, leaving Hugel and his lawyers only the weekend to obtain and study the Brother International records.

The second meeting, held on Monday, did not persuade the *Post* to hold the story. It did agree to print a boxed statement of denial by Hugel along with the story. The long *Post* article, written by its star investigative reporter, Bob Woodward, and Patrick Tyler, ran to 150 column-inches plus a secondary biographical piece on Hugel. It appeared on July 14. Its overall effect was devastating to Hugel. Quotations selected from the tapes created the impression that he was pursuing the McNells for the money owed him with single-minded, foul-mouthed ruthlessness. The article failed to mention, however, that the taped conversations from which it quoted liberally had all taken place between September 13 and November 22, 1974, *after* the McNell firm had ceased working for Brother; that, in fact, the SEC had suspended the McNell firm from all trading on September 13, 1974; that Hugel had severed all personal and legal relations with the McNells two days later; and that McNell Securities had gone into bankruptcy soon after.

While the *Post* story did note that "the McNells have not been available for further comment since last week," there was no mention of the probable cause: that they were on the lam for fear the authorities might charge them with larceny!

Less than three months after the *Post's* story about Hugel was published, the *Wall Street Journal* reported that Triad Energy Corp. and Everest Petroleum, Inc., oil- and gas-exploration firms the McNells had headed, had filed suit in federal court against the brothers, alleging they had helped themselves to $3 million of the two companies' funds.[77]

As it turned out, when the federal court subsequently found for the corporate plaintiffs and against the McNells, the brothers—in the weeks preceding their conversations with the

Post—had been funeling money from Triad and Everest into their personal trading accounts. This, rather than any fear arising from the publication of the Hugel story (they told Woodward they feared for their lives), is the likely reason for their disappearance immediately after the story's publication.

Does the apparently uncritical acceptance of the McNells' charges by the *Post* mean that the newspaper was out to get Hugel? That would be for the courts to decide in the event Hugel were to sue the *Post* for libel. He would, of course, have to prove that the Post acted with malicious intent, a difficult thing to prove.*

So far as legal action is concerned, Hugel decided to go after the McNells. Once the story was published, he quickly realized he could not fight the accusations against him and perform his official duties effectively, so he resigned from the CIA. He then turned his full energy to fighting the allegations and reestablishing himself in private business.

On November 3, 1982, Hugel filed a defamation-of-character suit against the McNells in the United States District Court in New Hampshire. The brothers, hiding from the law by that time, did not defend the suit. Hugel obtained a default judgment on February 24, 1983. The court not only found in his favor, but it also widened the legal "discovery" process** available to Hugel in his pursuit of damages from the McNells. This meant that he could subpoena *Washington Post* executive editor Ben Bradlee and reporters Woodward and Tyler.

The court did not award damages until September 1984. Meanwhile, Hugel experienced the same kind of media fallout from his resignation that Richard Allen had been experiencing. When stories about his reentry into the business world were

*In 1982, a jury awarded Mobil Oil Corp. president William Tavoulareas a $2.2 million libel award against the *Post* and reporter Tyler. The judge reversed the decision because he could find no evidence of "knowing lies" on the newspaper's part; however, he said of the story that it "falls short of being a model of fair, unbiased investigative journalism."

**Evidence gathered in depositions, under oath.

published they invariably carried a notation that he had resigned in the face of accusations of wrongdoing.

Hugel and his attorneys, Perito, Duerk & Pinto of Washington, sought corrections and retractions promptly in each case. They obtained a number of them, including an "Editors Notes" item in the *New York Times* clarifying a March 12, 1984 story that had made the point that Hugel had resigned from the CIA "amid questioning of his private business dealings." The clarifying story explained the McNell allegations, Hugel's denial, the fact the McNells were sought by the Federal Bureau of Investigation and that Hugel had never been charged by any government agency.

Each time Hugel obtained a published clarification or apology he sent reprints to a mailing list of friends and supporters. This showed them that he was fighting back on the legal front and talking back to the media at the same time.

Hugel obtained a major vindication on September 20, 1984 when federal magistrate William Barry awarded him $931,000 in expenses and damages from the McNells as a result of the defamation suit. In his order, Judge Barry commented that "neither the financial information nor the loan were given [to the McNells] to affect the market of Brother International stock."

Judge Barry also commented on the *Post's* 1981 story and its aftermath. He wrote:

> I do take into consideration that the plaintiff is a hard-nosed businessman who beat a swift retreat from Washington in spite of the fact that the CIA offered him administrative leave to fight the false accusations.
>
> As could be expected, the matter lost its newsworthiness and the frequency of articles tapered off quickly. The plaintiff then spent his time getting himself together and reentering the business world. In 1983 the plaintiff attempted to return to the public arena and accepted a position as an unpaid liaison between the State of New Hampshire and Washington. He also became actively involved with the reconstruction of Rockingham Racetrack. The plaintiff's efforts to reenter public

life by accepting the liaison position and becoming involved in the quasi-development of Rockingham Racetrack have been met by his political opponents with republication of the defamatory statements and the observation that he left the CIA while under fire.

Judge Barry went on to note that when Edwin Meese III was nominated in early 1984 to be U.S. attorney general, "Because of the plaintiff's [Hugel's] close association with Mr. Meese in the presidential campaign, the whole matter received another round in the press with renewed intensity."

The judge's order also noted, with some irony, how such reverberations in the media can be compounded in the political arena: "...the plaintiff's name, along with others, is being used by Democratic presidential hopefuls as examples of President Reagan's appointees that have been forced to resign because of illegal and unethical conduct. And so the defamation goes on."

Both Allen and Hugel proved the value of fighting back and talking back when accused of wrongdoing from which they had been cleared. Had they not fought back, they would have faced the prospect of the media repeating indefinitely the original accusations without reporting their vindications.

The Westmoreland Case

When he saw a promotional spot on CBS television one morning in January 1982 for a documentary titled "The Uncounted Enemy: A Vietnam Deception," retired Army Chief of Staff Gen. William C. Westmoreland picked up the telephone. He called a Washington friend, Dave Henderson, a public relations/public affairs specialist. "The general called me that morning, very upset, and said something to the effect that 'they are going to try to make me look like a criminal and I don't know what to do about it.'"[78]

Henderson recommended that the general hold a news conference. Since Westmoreland had no staff, Henderson offered to put it together at no charge. Westmoreland then began calling old associates from Vietnam days to ask them to join him at the news conference.

The next day he had cause to be further upset. CBS ran a full-page promotional ad in several large newspapers for the forthcoming broadcast under the headline, "CONSPIRACY."

The program itself was strong stuff. As it opened, Mike Wallace told viewers that CBS would present "evidence of what we have come to believe was a conscious effort—indeed a conspiracy at the highest levels of American military intelligence—to suppress and alter critical intelligence on the enemy in the year leading up to the Tet offensive."

CBS' thesis was that U.S. military headquarters in Saigon had systematically underestimated enemy strength in order to put a good face on things back home, with the result that the U.S. Army was unprepared when the offensive came and the American public was unprepared psychologically.

Central to the thesis is the belief that the Tet offensive was a major loss for the United States. It was perceived that way by most media people covering it at the time. Because this perception became so widespread in the United States (television being a particularly persuasive medium), the Tet offensive did turn out to be a watershed event. It can be argued that U.S. public support began to erode seriously from this point onward.

Yet, at the time, Gen. Westmoreland claimed that Tet was a military victory for the United States. Indeed, a founder of the Vietnam National Liberation Front, Truong Nho Tang, later wrote that Tet had cost them half their forces and had proved catastrophic to their planning.

CBS stuck to the popular view and, in the broadcast, revived old differences between army analysts in Saigon and CIA analysts in Washington over the size of the communist forces and the rate of their infiltration down the Ho Chi Minh Trail. The CIA estimated approximately 500,000 in standing forces; Gen. Westmoreland's staff reported 300,000 or fewer. As to the monthly infiltration rate leading up to the 1968 Tet offensive, official estimates from the field never went above 6,000, yet CIA analysts estimated up to 20,000.

The difference of some 200,000 in standing forces lay in interpretation. Westmoreland was most concerned about the main enemy forces, and considered the others to be "punji-stick paramilitary types—young guerrillas in training and partisan village elders, women and children."[79]

CBS interviewed Westmoreland for the program, but he came off poorly in the edited portions shown. Beside Westmoreland, CBS interviewed an array of seemingly expert witnesses including one, Sam Adams, a former CIA analyst who, it turns out, had been a paid adviser to CBS for the program. The overall effect via the cool, impressionistic medium of television was that Westmoreland looked bad and the conspiracy theory looked good.

Three days later, Westmoreland held his news conference in Washington, with several former colleagues standing with him, including retired Lt. Gen. Daniel O. Graham, former head of the Defense Intelligence Agency and the only former colleague to defend Westmoreland in the CBS program.

Westmoreland came out swinging in his opening statement. He and his wife had just been to see the movie *Absence of Malice*, he said. "Although I did not take the movie literally, it did show an innocent man whose life—and many others'—were ruined by unscrupulous use of the media. Little did I know that within a week a real-life, notorious reporter, Mike Wallace, would try to prosecute me in a star-chamber procedure with distorted, false and specious information....It was all there: the arrogance, the color, the drama, the contrived plot, the close shots—everything but the truth."[80]

Accuracy in Media (AIM), the conservative media watchdog organization, soon took up Westmoreland's case, but it was an article in *TV Guide* by Sally Bedell and Don Kowet that began to turn the tables on CBS. The article, "Anatomy of a Smear: How CBS News Broke the Rules and 'Got' Gen. Westmoreland," was based on internal CBS materials leaked by network employees. It cast doubt on the motives of those who developed the program.

In a subsequent article in the *Washington Journalism Review*, Kowet went into more detail, quoting a memo from CBS producer George Crile following the taping of an interview with paid consultant Sam Adams. The memo, to Wallace, reads: "The Adams interview was not only a terrific interview, it looks beautiful. Now all you have to do is break General Westmoreland and we have the whole thing aced."[81]

The Bedell-Kowet article in *TV Guide* claimed that CBS had coached interviewees who agreed with its thesis, and ignored a number of sources who would have supported Gen. Westmoreland. The heat was turning up. The president of CBS News, Van Gordon Sauter, ordered an internal investigation.

The executive appointed to this task, Burton Benjamin, reported his findings in July 1982. He concluded that "a 'conspiracy,' given the accepted definition of the word, was not proved." Sauter released a summary of the investigator's report, both the favorable and unfavorable aspects, but concluded that "we support the substance of the broadcast."

This satisfied neither CBS' not Westmoreland's supporters. Westmoreland asked for 45 minutes of air time; CBS offered 15. The negotiations broke down. On September 13, Gen. Westmoreland filed a $120 million lawsuit against CBS. His suit charged that the CBS promotional spots and newspaper ad, the program itself and the Sauter postinvestigation memo had been created with "knowledge that they were false, unfair, inaccurate and defamatory."

The preliminary battles leading to the trial in October 1984 were bitterly fought because at stake was the general's access to CBS' footage on the cutting room floor, the edited materials not used in the program. Westmoreland won access in what may prove to be a landmark skirmish in media lawsuits.

After nearly five months, a parade of witnesses for both sides and extensive coverage by the media, print and broadcast, the Westmoreland-CBS lawsuit was settled out of court. Funds were running out for the general, and adverse testimony by some of his former colleagues seemed to put the handwriting on the wall: The jury was not going to find CBS guilty of malice. In settling, both sides claimed victory, Westmoreland because he had fully aired the issue; CBS because it had escaped a possible judgment and worn down the other side. While Westmoreland got no money in the settlement, CBS, for its part, agreed to absorb all of its legal costs.

There were hosannas throughout the media world for what was described as a victory for the First Amendment, as if a libel verdict would imperil the First Amendment. Perhaps the greatest benefit of the trial will be that CBS and the other networks will take greater care in preparing future documentaries.

Libel Cases: A High Success Ratio

As was noted in Chapter One, a high percentage of libel verdicts (85 percent according to Stanford University law professor Marc Franklin) favor plaintiffs. Scholars worry that public confidence in the news media will continue to erode if something is not done to reverse this trend. Fred Friendly says we must find a better way for aggrieved parties to talk back to the media.

Friendly makes the point that there is total confusion over the concept of "malice." He makes the point that once a jury has satisfied itself that malice has been committed by a journalist or media organization, it concludes "the journalist deserves a spanking." The jury proceeds to award not only compensatory damages for actual monetary losses, but also punitive damages that may amount to millions of dollars. Friendly says, "...the upshot is that we now fine people for exercising their First Amendment rights—just what the First Amendment was supposed to prevent."[82]

Friendly argues that juries are conscientious about trying to reach a proper verdict on the facts, but are hard-pressed to make an even-handed determination of damages, especially punitive ones. He notes that over 70 percent of the libel verdicts carrying punitive damages have the fines reduced or eliminated on appeal. He says the only winners in these battles are the lawyers.

He says that the solution is simple, but may be hard to implement: The courts need to clarify what constitutes journalistic excess and journalists need to be more open to the idea of providing media access to people who feel they have been mistreated.

Earlier in this chapter we examined a number of ways of talking back to the media short of the extreme of a libel suit. Fred Friendly probably did not have President Reagan in mind when he advocated more media access for aggrieved parties, but the President didn't hesitate to seek direct access one evening in 1982. When he felt his position on an issue had been inaccurately portrayed on the "CBS Evening News" on August 17 that year, Reagan picked up the phone and called Dan Rather—while the news was still being shown.

It began this way. Early in the newscast Rather said:

> President Reagan has a big, new fight on his hands tonight on top of the one he's already having over passage of his $99 billion tax increase bill.
>   The new fight: China. Mr. Reagan's decision today to tilt away from Taiwan and more toward the mainland Chinese. He has decided to limit arms sales to Taiwan, sales the Peking government refused to abide. Taken together, Mr. Reagan has now reversed the policy and infuriated conservative members of his own party on two scores. First, the tax increases, now, China.

The newscast moved into footage about the tax issue, then a report on the China matter. During this time, President Reagan phoned Rather. Following the "tax" and "China" stories, Rather reported to his audience:

> An unusual thing happened here in our newsroom tonight. The President of the United States telephoned. He did so after seeing and hearing what you just did—our reports about Taiwan and mainland China. He watched the first of our broadcasts. You are watching the second.

The President said that he was concerned and upset about the general coverage on this story. Mr. Reagan told me, and I quote, "There has been no retreat by me, no change whatsoever. We will continue to arm Taiwan. I am bound by and will obey the Taiwan [Relations] Act." And, continuing to quote President Reagan, "We have a moral obligation to Taiwan. I am concerned," said President Reagan, "about the possible harm these reports may do to our international relations." End of quotation. That was the telephone call, President Reagan to our newsroom just a few moments ago.

That worked for the President of the United States. It may not for you. If the local evening news seems to distort your organization's position on an issue, you may not get the newscast interrupted by a telephone call to the anchorman or anchorwoman, but the Reagan call underscores the importance of taking prompt action if you intend to talk back to the media effectively.

Part Three
GETTING
HELP

9/ Crises: Avoiding Them and Managing Them

Some companies live constantly with potential danger: public utilities, mining companies, oil and gas refiners and processors—to name a few. Most of them have standby plans for dealing with crises and disasters, but what happens if your company is in a field of business where crises are unlikely to occur and goes for years without any serious accidents? Even if you never expect a crisis or disaster and have little idea of what form it might take if one befell your organization, you can still have the rudiments of a crisis management plan at hand. The rudiments include:

1. Designation of a single spokesperson with one or more deputies if needed. The chain of command must be known by all concerned.

2. Determination by management to respond calmly, even if consultations among members of the crisis management team must be hasty prior to the spokesperson's facing the media.
3. A commitment to be straightforward with the media.

Johnson & Johnson's response to the widely publicized Tylenol poisonings in the Chicago area in 1982 has often been cited as a model for company behavior under crisis circumstances. Johnson & Johnson's McNeill Laboratories subsidiary, makers of Tylenol, quickly pulled the product off the shelves and did not return it until a new tamper-proof package had been developed. Meanwhile, Johnson & Johnson and McNeill officials were open to the media, responding to interview requests both at the time of intense news coverage during the crisis and later when Tylenol was ready to be put back on the market. The story had a happy ending for the pharmaceutical manufacturer: By mid-1984 Tylenol's share of the market was nearly back to where it had been before the poisoning cases occurred.

Less well known are the "copycat" cases that followed the Tylenol tampering. For a small company, such as Hygrade Food Products Corp. of Southfield, Michigan, a crisis with the potentiality for corporate disaster can hit with the random suddenness of a cyclone.

HYGRADE AND THE MYSTERIOUS RAZOR BLADE

Hygrade is not a large company. Its annual sales are in the $200 million range. While it sells a full line of processed meats, its staple is frankfurters. In fact, it makes the nation's second most popular brand, Ball Park. In its home market area of Detroit, however, Ball Park is a strong Number One.

Hygrade prided itself on turning out good products in an atmosphere of positive labor relations and good working conditions.

Imagine management's consternation when, in late October 1982, it was flooded with reports by Detroit area consumers who claimed they had found foreign objects in Ball Park frankfurters. In all, there were 14 such reports before the crisis reached its climax and was solved.

Charles Ledgerwood, Hygrade's operations vice president, learned of the first report of an adulterated Ball Park frank from a *Detroit News* reporter on Wednesday, October 28 while on a business trip to Chicago. The reporter had tracked him down to tell him that a Detroit housewife, Shirley Watson, had claimed she discovered a razor blade in a Ball Park frank she had taken fresh from the package.

Two thoughts crossed Ledgerwood's mind. A piece of metal from plant machinery might somehow have chipped off and gotten into the frank, or a disgruntled employee might have sabotaged the package. He told the reporter he would look into the matter at once and would call him back. He returned immediately to Detroit.

The next morning, Ledgerwood called on the woman and found that the foreign object in the frankfurter was half of a Gillette Blue Blade. Thus, chips from plant machinery were ruled out. Ledgerwood reported his findings to company president Clyde Riley. They quickly made two decisions that proved to be crucial—and positive—for Hygrade: They decided to be open with the media and they decided Hygrade would have a single spokesman, Ledgerwood, for the duration of the crisis.

They made another decision, too, that proved to be a mistake. As Ledgerwood later recalled, "When we saw the tampered product, we knew it couldn't have been done in a store. We did not consider that the consumer might have done it."[83] This line of reasoning led them to the supposition that the tampering case was the result of a disgruntled—and probably demented—employee who had sabotaged Mrs. Watson's package of franks. On the strength of this reasoning the company issued a press release acknowledging Mrs. Watson's "discovery" and blaming "deliberate sabotage by a misguided employee."[84]

This approach had three faults: Management's theory was dead wrong, as it turned out; the announcement actually encouraged more "copycat" tamperings; and, not least of all, it hurt employee morale, which had always been high.

The media amplified both the consumer's claim and Hygrade's response. The story led the television news in the Detroit area that evening. Within two days there were so many reports of razor blades, nails and other objects found in Ball Park franks that Hygrade stopped production at its Livonia, Michigan plant and recalled all of its franks—350,000 pounds of them—from area stores.

As the news of the reports spread, the atmosphere at Hygrade became "one of fear—support, but fear," according to Riley.[85] Ledgerwood said he "feared for the company's existence."[86]

By Friday, Riley and Ledgerwood began to doubt their "disgruntled employee" theory. Instead, they began to suspect a series of hoaxes. All of the dangerous objects found in the Ball Park franks were slightly different from one another. And, because the Ball Park packages are age-dated, management realized that some of the objects, had they been inserted at the plant, would have begun corroding by the time they were "discovered" and reported by the customers. Yet none were corroded.

Riley and Ledgerwood did not take their new suspicions to the media just yet. First, Ledgerwood gathered the employees together. The previous day he had done the same thing, to announce the "disgruntled employee" theory. This time, he says, "When I found we had been wrong, I assembled them again and told them about the mistake and apologized. They rallied around and then volunteered to come in on the weekend and inspect all those packages."[87] Even retired Hygrade employees joined in the inspection effort.

On Saturday, while workers were going over thousands of packages of Ball Park franks with metal detectors, the company got a break. One woman who had reported finding a razor blade in a frank the day before failed a lie detector test and then admitted that her claim was a hoax.

By Sunday afternoon, Hygrade's workers had inspected 300,000 franks and found no metal in them. At that point, Ledgerwood announced his findings, the woman's confession and management's conclusion that all the reports were hoaxes.

The media, having swooped down on the first "discovery" story and Hygrade's response, now turned around and played the "hoax" story as strongly as the original one. There were no more reports of foreign objects in Ball Park franks.

All of this happened over a five-day period, from Wednesday to Sunday. About a month later, Livonia, where Hygrade's main plant is located, staged a Livonia Loves Hygrade Week. The goal was for its citizens to consume 140,000 pounds of Ball Park franks that week. The final tally was 148,000. The closeness continues. According to Ledgerwood, "We are far more active in the community than we were before the incident."[88]

About the ordeal itself, Ledgerwood is philosophical. "We had no lasting negatives. Rather, we had some positive results. Business is actually up from the time before the tampering cases."[89]

Ledgerwood contends that companies that make "tamperable" products should review their product security procedures at regular intervals.

Taking legal action against hoaxers is not worthwhile, he says. Most of the perpetrators had only modest means; indeed, the apparent motive behind the hoaxes was to shake money out of Hygrade. The company could have sued the hoaxers, but did not. Suing, they reasoned, would have produced only Pyrrhic victories. The verdicts would have been technically satisfying, but they would not have compensated Hygrade for the approximately $1 million the crisis cost it and, along with the trials, there would have been daily media reminders of the original razor blade and nail scare.

Laws for dealing with product tamperers were weak in this instance. Except for the misdemeanor offense of filing a false police report, the hoaxers apparently broke no laws. One of them spent 10 days in jail. Nothing happened to the others.

Ledgerwood has some other observations about the crisis, in retrospect: "The media treated us right; our customers treated us fairly; our retailers went overboard to help us recover; and our employees stood behind us."[90]

EARLY DETECTION

Careful monitoring of issues that may affect your company can result in containing a problem before it reaches crisis proportions, provided you act on the information you have acquired.

The public relations director of a large bank took strong action that may have solved such a problem. In the debate in the United States over South Africa's controversial apartheid policy, efforts have been made to persuade states, colleges and universities and various other institutional investors to disinvest their holdings in banks and corporations that do business in South Africa. Most U.S. corporations doing business in that country adhere to a code of standards called The Sullivan Principles. This has resulted in progressive economic improvements for black employees. Advocates of the policy of disinvestment have tended to ignore this, however, and continue to pursue the policy, apparently in the belief that it will cause U.S. companies to pull out, to be followed by the collapse of the South African economy and government—events that are unlikely to happen.

When Harvard University's trustees began to vote in favor of disinvestment, they included the bank alluded to above. The bank's public relations director showed that two could play the same game. He "talked back" to a Harvard medium by canceling the bank's advertising in the *Harvard Business Review*. "I figured that if our investment return to Harvard was comprised of 'evilly gotten' money, the same must hold true of our advertising dollars and that their magazine would not want to be tainted," he said.[91]

PREVENTION

Herbert Schmertz, vice president of public affairs of the Mobil Corporation, has guided Mobil's highly visible editorial-style advertising program since its adoption in 1970. To date, more than 600 ads have appeared on newspaper op-ed pages and in news and opinion magazines. Among those regularly carrying the ads are *Time*, the *Wall Street Journal*, *New York Times*, *Washington Post*, *Los Angeles Times*, *Chicago Tribune*, *Boston Globe* and *Atlanta Constitution*.

Schmertz says that Mobil's reasoning behind the advocacy ads is "our inability to communicate with the American public in words of our own choosing, without going through the filters of the media."[92]

The original motivation for the ads seems to have been a combination of that frustration expressed by Schmertz, coupled with a desire to build a positive image for the company in an atmosphere that was increasingly hostile to large oil companies. Today Mobil, perhaps more than any other large oil company, has nurtured public goodwill both through its advocacy ads and its extensive program of grants to the arts and public television drama.

According to Schmertz, back in 1970 "it seemed that enormous external forces were already buffeting our company and our industry. We believed these forces would do enormous and irreparable damage unless we recognized their existence and attempted to counter them."[93] As the forces he had in mind, Schmertz cited the rise of environmentalism, consumerism, politicians and the press.

Out of this concern came the Mobil advocacy advertising program that, in its early days, ran under the name "Observations." Each ad contained several short subjects. Later, the format was changed to resemble a newspaper editorial, although it was clearly a paid advertisement and carried the Mobil sig at the bottom. Headlines such as "Let's Not Tax Away Incentives" (opposing new taxes on decontrolled oil), "A Cup For

You to Fill" (urging voluntary support of community activities) and "The Customers Always Write" (about reader response to the ads) typify the editorial-style campaign. All of the ads are staff written.

The target audience for the Mobil ads is a group usually described as "opinion leaders" in major cities. This includes public officeholders, business and industry leaders, media commentators, academics, scientists, community leaders—and those who advise such people.

After nearly 15 years of the ads, does Schmertz believe his early premise that Mobil needed to go around the media "filters" is still valid? "Yes, absolutely," he says.[94]

"I'm not interested in talking back to the media. I am interested in talking direct to the American people. If I can do that through the media, fine. If not, I'll find another way. I am interested in being a responsible critic of the media," he added.

"The media consider themselves as surrogates of the public," Schmertz says. "This is a myth. If they have tried to be that they have failed."

In contending that print media are the best carriers for an advocacy message (few broadcast outlets accept advocacy advertising), Schmertz made the point that "we view our ads as pamphlets in the Thomas Paine tradition, and we view newspapers and magazines as a delivery system."[95]

KEEPING BAD NEWS FROM BECOMING A CRISIS

About the last thing a manager wants to have to do is to lay off a good part of the work force or, worse, close the plant. Yet this happens, even in good times, as America's industrial patterns adjust to a changing world.

If the economics of the situation dictate closing down a plant, moving it or cutting back its work force, the decision to take one of these steps will have been part of a process and not a surprise to management. Therefore, it should not be a surprise to the plant's work force or the community.

Shocks and surprises that bring negative news almost always bring negative, angry responses. In the case of plant closures or moves, this can turn out to be very costly for the company. Increasingly, dislocated workers are going to court to sue. Labor unions, if caught by surprise, will fight back furiously. And the media are almost certain to paint the company as uncaring and insensitive.

Instead, as the process leading toward a painful decision moves forward, the manager should set out to cushion the potential bad news that may lie ahead by sharing with the work force and the media the data that show that the plant's business is not all it should be, and that closure or reduced operations may be in the cards. This should be coupled with a well-conceived plan to help affected workers. That plan, in turn, must be put into action concurrent with the closure announcement. Consider the following three recent case histories.

In November 1982, when the U.S. auto industry was still being battered by recession, Ford Motor Co. announced it would close its Milpitas, California assembly plant. Some 2,800 jobs would disappear. Ford had prepared the workers for the announcement during a series of weekly information sessions with management. "...[T]he announcement was so well received that we opened the plant for a public tour that day as planned," said Hal Axtell, the industrial relations manager.[96]

The closure announcement and outplacement process involved several elements. Ford gave the employees six months advance warning of the closing. It assembled a $6.7 million retraining and outplacement program. It offered courses in skills such as welding and computer operation. As part of the outplacement program, the company held seminars on resume writing and it videotaped mock interviews to help workers sharpen their interview skills. Both company and union officials consider the Milpitas closing a good example of labor-management cooperation.

Another company, Atari, did not fare so well as far as employee morale is concerned. In early 1983, its way of announcing that it was eliminating 600 jobs in a California plant was simply to call the workers off their jobs and hand them pink slips.

Curtiss-Wright showed similar insensitivity when 400 workers at its Wood-Ridge, New Jersey jet engine facility were notified they were losing their jobs. They read about it on the bulletin board at the end of the day's shift. "'They should have treated us like human beings,' moaned one employee to a local newspaper."[97] That is the kind of negative public relations no company wants.

In the case of plant reductions, closures or proposed moves, talking early to the media as well as to the plant work force takes the place of talking back later.

10/ Watchdogs

Any executive or organization that has been the subject of what seemed to be a slanted or error-filled story in the news media may have longed for a neutral party—a sort of cosmic fact-finding committee—to set the record straight once and for all. Alas, no such omniscient or omnipotent person or group exists. Still, there have been—and are—groups and mechanisms intended to deal with media bias and fairness. They have met with varying degrees of success, as we shall see in this chapter.

THE WATCHDOG THAT DID NOT BARK

On March 23, 1984 the National News Council (NNC), by a vote of nine to three, decided to shut down at the end of that month, after 11 years of seeking to find a niche for itself as America's evenhanded media watchdog. The council came into being because of concerns by some in the media about increasing attacks on media "negativism" (e.g., then Vice President Spiro Agnew's famous speech with its memorable line accusing the media of being "nattering nabobs of negativism"). It died because of suspicion and lack of support from the very people it was attempting to protect—journalists.

A funeral notice in the *Columbia Journalism Review* put it this way: "Those who kept the National News Council going were not easily discouraged. They persevered through 11 years of under-financing, hostility from major news organizations and professional suspicion before closing up shop...."[98]

The NNC began life in 1973 with high hopes. Its brochure described it as "an independent, non-governmental organization established to serve the public interest in 1) providing a forum through which any individual or organization can present a complaint when it is felt an injustice has been done because of inaccurate and/or unfair reporting of the news; 2) upholding the principles of the free press guarantee of the First Amendment; and 3) studying and reporting on issues relating to press policies and ethics."

The council's method was to examine and rule on complaints brought to it by persons or organizations who felt they had been wronged by news organizations. Complainants had to agree to waive legal action in order for the NNC to consider the case. Thus, the council saw itself as an alternative to the libel suit. Had its findings been widely publicized, it might have succeeded.

As it was, the council, armed with high principles, considered more than 1,000 formal complaints and acted on 242 of them. It was not an easy job. The NNC always acted as a committee of the whole, and getting its 18 members together to devote the necessary time to hearing testimony and ruling on a case involved complicated scheduling negotiations.

A more difficult problem, and one that hastened the council's demise, was the unwillingness of the news media to promote its findings. Richard Salant, the NNC's last president and chief ex-ecutive officer (and retired president of CBS News) worked energetically to correct this problem, but with little success. He also worked for no pay and ran an organization with a puny budget of $300,000 a year in makeshift space near Lincoln Center on New York's Upper West Side.

The basic problem was resistance to the council concept from the top. According to Salant, in a 1983 interview, "the *New York Times* has long resisted the concept of the National News Council. Our business—journalism—follows the leader and the leader is the *New York Times*. The *Times* sees no need for the NNC. They seem to think it is a first step in a process leading to government interference. The *Columbia Journalism Review* used to carry our findings, but they dropped them a few years ago on the grounds they had 'no space' for them any longer."[99]

The NNC, which derived 29 percent of its financial support from media organizations, 25 percent from corporations, 4 percent from individuals and 42 percent from foundations, was not mourned by the leader of the journalism field. Arthur Ochs Sulzberger, publisher of the *New York Times*, declined to comment on the council's decision to go out of business.[100]

Salant felt that a restructuring of the council's membership might have prolonged it. From the beginning, it had 10 members from the public sector and eight from the media. He felt that a split of 12 media members and six "public" members would have resulted in greater acceptance by the media of the council's work. He made the point that media people will more readily accept criticism from their peers than from outsiders, and that they tend to be resistant to criticism from people whom they consider lacking in qualifications (i.e., experience in or understanding of the news business). Skeptics need not have been fearful, as it turned out. The NNC rejected nearly 80 percent of the complaints it took up. The watchdog never got a chance to bark.

THE WATCHDOG THAT BARKS NONSTOP

Accuracy in Media—AIM—was born a few years before the National News Council, in 1969. Today, it is not only alive and well but is barking at media transgressions on a daily basis.

The same thing that led to the birth of the NNC—concern over media negativism—led to AIM's founding by Reed Irvine and a handful of friends. Both organizations were born of frustration, but stemming from different perceptions. The founders of the National News Council worried that charges of negativism were a reaction from reportage of Watergate and the Vietnam war and would get worse if an orderly mechanism were not set up for hearing specific complaints. Their ultimate concern was that generalized attacks on the media would escalate in the absence of such a mechanism, and might lead to erosion of First Amendment rights and to government interference with the media.

AIM's founders had a much different view. Founder Irvine, when asked what prompted its formation, replied, "Irresponsible journalism was an important factor. You will remember the turmoil on the college campuses and the serious riots in our cities in the late 1960s. It seemed to some of us that the news media were pouring gasoline on the flames by giving an extraordinary amount of publicity to the agitators. Many of the demonstrations reported on the nightly news were really media events. They wouldn't have occurred without the presence of the mass media."[101]

Television coverage of the turbulence surrounding the 1968 Democratic convention was the event that actually triggered AIM. Irvine, in elaborating on its beginnings, said, "I was chairman of a monthly luncheon group. We were finding ourselves frequently complaining about the media, especially television coverage of that convention. I found myself writing to the networks, urging them to police themselves. They showed no interest, so we decided to form a group to monitor coverage. A friend volunteered to put up $200 and that was our starting budget."[102]

Today, AIM has more than 30,000 dues-paying members and an annual budget of $1.4 million. For their $15-a-year dues, members get a lively semimonthly newsletter documenting current cases against the media from a watchdog that barks nonstop.

Irvine, a retired Federal Reserve System economist, says that "AIM's purpose is to encourage greater accuracy, fairness and integrity in the news media by calling attention to specific cases of distortion and unfairness. We try to bring pressure to correct such situations."[103]

Just as Spiro Agnew's speech prompted the NNC's founders to get organized, it inspired AIM, but in a different way. Referring to the Agnew speech, Irvine said, "I felt we had to go to specific examples, not generalizations as he did."[104] And that is what Irvine and his staff have been doing ever since. Today, in addition to its newsletter, AIM turns out a weekly column that runs in approximately 100 newspapers and on a five-day-a-week radio commentary broadcast over 60 stations. Irvine also says his organization writes "lots of letters" to editors. The organization maintains a list of newspapers that syndicate major columnists. "When we need to do a corrective letter in response to a column, we mail the same letter to every newspaper on that columnist's list," says Irvine.[105]

AIM does not scatter its effort over hundreds of cases; instead, it handles perhaps two or three dozen a year. "It is easier to go into depth than to capsulize. You can be more careful when you handle fewer cases," Irvine says.[106]

Dr. Edward Teller, the famed nuclear physicist, brought a case to AIM in 1983 and received the kind of careful attention Irvine speaks about. On April 28 of that year, Teller testified before the House Armed Services Committee about the need for a strategic antimissile defense system. As he put it later in a letter to AIM members:

> When I gave my testimony I was pleased to be able to deliver a positive message of hope. I told the committee that President Reagan was on the right track in proposing that we develop an antimissile defense system. As a scientist with long experience in this field and a consultant at the Lawrence Livermore laboratories, I was able to say that President Reagan's proposal was sound, both in theory and in fact. It was important that this

be said, since many of the "experts" who "inform" the public through our newspapers and on television were ridiculing the president's proposal as "Star Wars" fantasy.

Teller's "positive message of hope" that day never made it to the news media. Instead, when the reporters crowded around him after he gave his testimony, all they wanted to know about was his reaction to that morning's *New York Times* story.

The *Times* story reported that Teller had been involved in the preparation of President Reagan's March 23 speech proposing a strategic defense initiative. It also said he had received, as a gift, a large amount of stock in Helionetics, Inc., a company that could produce lasers that might be used as a weapon in space against missiles. From all of this a reader might infer that Teller had prompted the President to plug the strategic defense initiative because a company in which he, Teller, was a shareholder would benefit from adoption of such a system. Since the *Times* also reported that Helionetics' stock price had gone up sharply the week before the President's speech, a reader might also infer that Teller had leaked the fact that the President was going to make his proposal.

It all tracked logically—except that none of it was true, according to Teller. In his letter to AIM members, he says that although he was an occasional White House adviser he was not involved in the March 23 Reagan speech and did not know about the strategic defense initiative's inclusion in the speech until shortly before it was delivered. He also notes that he bought his shares in Helionetics and did so while Jimmy Carter was president. He also points out that Helionetics does not produce a weapons laser. "It is working on a laser whose only military use is to communicate with submerged submarines," he said. He added that Helionetics' principal work is with solar energy.

Teller suspected that the timing of the *Times* story was less than a coincidence. He turned to Accuracy in Media. AIM did the following:

◆ Sent a letter to the *Times* detailing the story's errors.

- ◆ Covered the story in its newsletter, and in Irvine's newspaper column and his radio commentary, "Media Monitor."

- ◆ Ran a full-page ad in the *Wall Street Journal*—a first-person account of the situation by Teller—under the heading "I was NOT the Only Victim of the *New York Times*."

- ◆ Met on June 30 with *Times* chairman Arthur Ochs Sulzberger and vice chairman Sidney Gruson, to discuss this and other issues.

While the *Times* did not retract its original story's errors, it did report the fact that Teller had been cleared of possible conflict of interest by a White House investigation. That this fact was reported on p. 3 of the fourth section says something about the thinness of media executives' skin.

AIM concentrates much of its surveillance on the *New York Times*, the *Washington Post* and the three major commercial television networks because of their widespread national and international influence on public opinion. According to Irvine, AIM owns stock in the corporations that run these media heavyweights and in Time, Inc. "We go to their annual meetings and can question their chairmen directly. We can also submit shareholder resolutions, although this is getting more difficult because a recent SEC ruling has sharply increased the number of votes such a resolution must get in order to be resubmitted the next year. We are now studying the possibility of running some of our own candidates for directors on some of these corporate boards."[107]

Irvine, a deceptively mild-mannered, soft-spoken man, has no illusions about standing the media heavyweights on their heads with his corporate gadfly tactics; however, he believes that his activist approach keeps the other side on its toes and that things would be worse if AIM weren't around to tweak the noses of the heavyweights. AIM's brand of talking back to the media gets the kind of result that tickles Irvine's funny bone. In the organization's own brochure he quotes the *Washington Post*'s Ben Bradlee as saying of AIM, "You have revealed yourself as a miserable, carping retromingent vigilante."

If you are under media attack, will AIM help you? Irvine can't promise, but he says, "The sooner we hear about it, the better. Sometimes we can get something done almost immediately, with a phone call."[108] He cites a case that occurred one morning during the 1980 presidential campaign. CBS ran a television story listing issues on which Ronald Reagan had supposedly changed his stand. As the correspondent read each issue an "X" appeared over a picture of Reagan's face. Irvine, who thought this smacked of partisanship, called a CBS executive who seemed unruffled about the matter. Just the same, on that evening's 7 o'clock news, Walter Cronkite apologized for the "X-ing."

"This is our strength," says Irvine's colleague Bernie Yoh. "People have someone to call."[109] The number is (202) 783-4406.

OMBUDSMEN

Their titles may vary from newspaper to newspaper (reader editor, public editor, readers' representative), but they all answer to the generic title of "ombudsman" (a Swedish word). Most serve as watchdogs of the fairness, accuracy and balance of their own newspaper and field readers' complaints.

Today, less than 20 years after the first one was appointed by the *Louisville Courier-Journal* in 1967, 40 newspapers in the United States and Canada have ombudsmen. Impetus for the ombudsman movement came from a 1967 article by A.H. Raskin in the *New York Times* (which still does not have an ombudsman); according to an article on the ombudsman's role, in the *Columbia Journalism Review*, Raskin proposed that newspapers appoint "an ombudsman for the readers, armed with authority to get something done about valid complaints and to propose methods for more effective performance of the paper's service to the community."[110]

Despite these high principles, the movement has not been an unqualified success. Robert Haiman, former executive editor of the *St. Petersburg Times*, calls it "a sham."[111] His point is that the ombudsman insulates editors from readers, making the former less responsive to criticism than they should be. Alfred Jacoby, ombudsman of the *San Diego Union*, disagrees emphatically. He says that Haiman's view is "pure, unmitigated bullshit."[112] Yet Haiman did more than just voice his objections to the ombudsman system. He acted on it in 1980 by firing his paper's ombudsman and telling the switchboard operators to route complaint calls to the editors concerned.

Richard Cunningham, quoted in the same *Columbia Journalism Review* article, says Haiman is wrong. Cunningham was ombudsman of the *Minneapolis Tribune* for eight years, and is now editor of the monthly newsletter of the Organization of News Ombudsmen. He says that when editors receive complaints they think have little merit, they "immediately go into a bunch of defensive techniques."

Robert McCloskey, ombudsman for the *Washington Post* from late 1981 to late 1983, echoed this view. "There is a defensiveness and pettiness on the part of newspeople when their work is questioned. They are great about demanding that everyone else answer questions, but not so good at it themselves."[113]

The *Post*, which created the newspaper business' second ombudsman job in 1970, currently employs its seventh ombudsman, Sam Zagoria, who succeeded McCloskey when his two-year contract expired. (Traditionally, *Post* ombudsmen do not succeed themselves.) *Post* executive editor Ben Bradlee says that an ombudsman's importance lies in "influencing attitudes of reporters and editors by pointing up where we fall short of our goals."[114] But does it work that way? McCloskey says that "while newspapers are inching toward more responsibility and willingness to correct mistakes, there is a built-in resistance to acknowledging mistakes."[115] He adds, "Individual reputations can be quickly made for some [journalists]; play fast and loose with information but resent interference. Many are very thin-skinned. The younger people see ombudsmen as an intrusion."[116]

While most ombudsmen would concede that their activities do not result in major changes at their newspapers, they can play a positive role as sounding boards for readers. McCloskey received 50 to 60 reader letters a week during his two years at the *Post*. Cunningham, the former *Minneapolis Tribune* ombudsman, says that the ombudsman can identify patterns of complaints that would be difficult to spot if complaint calls were scattered throughout the news departments.

Typically, the ombudsman will write several memos to editors during any given week, commenting on errors or unbalanced accounts in news columns and sending on reader comments. Many, but not all, have their own columns. Most of these columns do not quarrel significantly with policies or major errors; rather, they run from discussions of inconsequential errors and minutiae to eye-glazing treatises on the role of the press in modern society.

While the ombudsmen's columns may be dull, their behind-the-scenes work may result in reporters and editors keeping on their toes. And earnestness is a mark of the ombudsman. "There is frustration," says McCloskey. "I am a one-man band in a very big newspaper. Much time is spent on the telephone, but this is important, because the least you can do is treat people courteously when they call."[117]

Donald Jones, ombudsman of the *Kansas City Star* and *Times*, underscores the importance of treating readers with respect. He says readers simply don't trust the media. He says the reasons are inaccuracy, arrogance and unfairness. He contends that factual errors do much to undermine reader confidence. He thinks readers see reporters and editors as a "privileged class," unwilling to admit mistakes. He also thinks readers are sophisticated enough to spot hatchet jobs quickly.[118]

Jones' own papers bend over backward to build reader confidence—judging from the box that appears on P. 2, showing the ombudsman's photo next to his title: readers' representative. It gives his telephone number and invites readers to call him if they have complaints or questions about news stories.

Some metropolitan dailies have developed alternatives to ombudsmen. At the *Oakland Tribune*, editor/publisher Robert Maynard, once a *Washington Post* ombudsman, has established community advisory boards, citizen groups that analyze the newspaper and suggest policy and story ideas.

The *Los Angeles Times* has a media reporter, David Shaw, instead of an ombudsman. Thus, it treats the media as a beat, like City Hall, business, education, and so forth. *Times* editor William Thomas thinks most ombudsmen are not hard enough on their own newspapers. "Most ombudsmen I've seen have let the paper off the hook. Their critiques appear on the op-ed page, which is for individual views, so the reader says, 'it's just his idea.'"[119]

While the debate among and between ombudsmen and editors about the value of the movement continues to swirl, ombudsmen still provide the person who has a complaint with one more avenue of expression. Former ombudsman McCloskey says, "If you're sending a letter to the editor in order to get your views on the record, also send a copy to the ombudsman. Chances are, he'll check back with the editor who, in turn, will probably check it with the reporter who wrote the story."[120]

REPLIES TO BROADCAST EDITORIALS

Strictly speaking, the broadcast editorial reply—on radio or television—is not a watchdog device, but it does provide you, as an individual or as a member of an organization that has a bone to pick with a station editorial, with an opportunity to be your own barking watchdog.

Jim Foy, director of editorials at KNBC-TV, NBC's owned-and-operated station in Los Angeles, says the process of getting on the air is not difficult if you have assembled your case well. "First, phone the station and ask for a copy of the editorial and express an interest in replying. Then, draft your reply and send it back to the station as soon as you possibly can," he says.[121]

How long should your commentary run? Some stations specify one-minute replies. Foy disagrees. "I think that's unreasonable to ask of people who don't write to time for a living, so we're more flexible. We say, 'write it for *about* one minute.'"[122]

Other rules of the road for broadcast editorial repliers:

1. Stick to the subject. Unlike the interview, where you can bridge over from a quick answer to the immediate question to some larger theme you want to put across, the broadcast editorial reply should avoid "taking off into the wild blue yonder on another subject," Foy says.

2. Be clear and conversational in tone. Remember, you are writing for the ear, not the eye, so don't draft a formal essay.

3. Dress for a television editorial reply as you would for an interview: simply. Neutral shade or dark suit or dress. No sharp contrasts. Avoid "vibrating" patterns such as plaids.

4. Will there be a TelePrompTer? Many stations use them, but inquire, should you be chosen to make a reply. Allow enough time to rehearse your reply several times with the TelePrompTer so your eyes won't be glued to a point above the viewer's line of vision. If the station does not use a TelePrompTer, put your reply in large letters on four-by-six-inch cards. Rehearse many times so that you will be able to look up and make eye contact with the camera.

5. Approach your subject as a protagonist, not an antagonist toward the audience or the station. "Remember," Foy says, "you are talking to someone's mother. Disagree, but don't be disagreeable. After all, you are trying to persuade people to agree with you."[123]

Editorial directors at radio and television stations often find they get several requests to reply to a given editorial. At Los Angeles' KNBC-TV, Foy says, "We try to connect the repliers, urging them to get together to sort things out and decide who will submit the reply. If it doesn't work out, we'll play referee."[124]

About one-third of those who telephone in to express interest in making an on-the-air reply drop off when they are asked to submit the reply in written draft form.

Of the approximately 3,000 television stations in the United States, some 250 broadcast editorials and replies with regularity. Typically, editorial time will be divided almost equally between editorials and replies in a given week. Many stations repeat editorials and replies two or three times.

Editorial director Foy points out that an enterprising protagonist for a particular issue may be a winner in one of two ways. "A great way to get important, controversial matters discussed is to try to sell your position on an issue to the editorial directors of your city's radio and television station," he says. "If they agree and editorialize on your side, fine. If they come down on the other side, then you get a crack at replying. Either way, your side gets the exposure it wants."[125]

Industries involved in controversial issues on a national scale can make good use of broadcast editorial replies locally, as well. By using electronic "clipping services" (such as Radio-TV Reports) to monitor editorials on stations in key markets, a trade association can be alerted to possibilities for editorial replies and use a local member to request the time and draft the reply. Even if the company or industry does not have a local representative to speak for it, it can send a videotape recording of a reply from headquarters for consideration. Timeliness is important, so call the distant station just as soon as you learn that it has editorialized on your subject.

Relatively few businesses and industries are capitalizing on this opportunity. Foy cites natural gas as a case in point. "I'm constantly astounded that the industry doesn't reply to editorials calling for regulated low prices," he says.[126]

11/ Helpers

Media trainer Dorothy Sarnoff says, "It's a mistake for a corporate executive to have a member of his staff rehearse him [for a media appearance]. No staff member wants to make the boss look bad by asking tough questions."[127] For this and other reasons—such as a desire to overcome nervousness—scores of business executives are enrolling in media techniques workshops or one-on-one training sessions with experts such as Sarnoff.

Today, many public relations firms provide media training for client executives. In addition, there are the specialists, such as Sarnoff, Shelley Klein and Ann Ready, whose principal business is media training. One firm, Jack Hilton, Inc., even offers a do-it-yourself training kit, consisting of a six-part, 210-minute collection of videotapes to help executives use television appearances more effectively. The cost for the kit is under $2,000, and the Hilton firm says it is used by nearly 100 companies.[128]

Media training programs are usually designed to cover more than one day, although some trainers will work with a small group of about six persons in a single four-hour session. Sarnoff offers three basic formats: a private course for individual executives divided into three two-hour sessions; a group course for up to 14, covering two full days, usually back-to-back; and intensive courses for specific media appearances. In the group courses, each participant is asked to bring two four-minute "hard business" talks in his or her field. The talk for the first day is supposed to inform; the one for Day Two is to persuade. Sarnoff videotapes each participant's presentation and plays it back while giving a critique.

Most media training sessions, private or group, work on the problem of executive nervousness, providing guidance on ways to relax before an audience or camera.

Some training programs will include "ambush" interviews of one or more members of the group as they break for lunch. This, too, is the subject of a critique later to see if the "victim" has effectively applied what he or she has learned in the earlier sessions.

Sarnoff, who claims to have started the whole media training phenomenon 16 years ago, is almost certainly the nation's champion in the size of her alumni group. She says that more than 60,000 persons have benefited from her training techniques over the years. Her firm, Speech Dynamics, based in New York City, is a subsidiary of an international advertising agency, Ogilvy and Mather.

Most media trainers will tailor a course to a particular executive's or group's requirements. Such subjects as the use of TelePrompTers, preparation for team presentations, delivery of impromptu talks, preparation for teleconferencing, and rehearsal and preparation for corporate annual meetings can be covered by most of the media training specialists.

The chief executive officer of one corporate client of my firm visits his media trainer before every major speech he gives, in order to polish his delivery. Another sent himself and all his top executives to a trainer before the introduction of his latest line of products to several hundred dealers. His company used a professional firm to produce the product introduction "show" in a large convention hall, right down to lighting, music and backdrops. Since the company was going to all that trouble, we recommended media training sessions and use of a TelePrompTer at the presentations—for the first time in the client company's history. The executive team's presentations were so well received by the dealers that the chief executive decided to go back to the trainer for more sessions that would lead to a program of speeches in civic forums in cities that are the company's major markets.

MRS—A SCIENCE INFORMATION CLEARINGHOUSE

In 1980, the year after the Three Mile Island nuclear power plant accident, the Scientists' Institute for Public Information, a New York-based nonprofit organization, decided to establish the Media Resource Service (MRS), a computerized file of some 15,000 names of scientists in virtually every scientific field. The service, which is available to all news media, seeks to provide balanced information from "scientists whose views reflect both sides—more frequently, all sides—of the question."[129]

The MRS recruits scientists to its information clearinghouse by reading current scientific literature and spotting names not already in its files; by sending out questionnaires; and by following through on recommendations of other scientists.

If a reporter calls for expert opinion on a controversial matter, the MRS will provide names and credentials of at least one expert on every side of the issue. The service itself takes no stand on issues, nor does it evaluate the merits of any member of its clearinghouse panel.

Would your company's staff scientist or consultant be eligible to be included in the clearinghouse? The MRS claims that it does not exclude anyone with credentials from its files. Presumably, your scientist's credentials would alert a reporter that he or she represents your company's point of view. Since the MRS will give the reporter names of scientists with other perspectives, the goal of "balance" is served. By offering the name of your scientist to the service, you help insure that your position will have exposure to the media.

The MRS keeps office hours from 8:30 A.M. to 7:00 P.M. (Eastern time) weekdays, and maintains a 24-hour, seven-day-a-week answering service that can page staff members during off-hours in case of need. Among its activities, the MRS acts as an honest broker in arranging interviews with scientists by inquiring media, often on short notice.

Is this honest-broker service widely used by the media? Yes, according to the service's 1983-84 tally of inquiries. It fielded, on an average, between 40 and 50 inquiries a week—more than 2,000 a year. Newspapers were the heaviest users (41.5 percent), with 237 inquiries ranging from the *Akron (Ohio) Beacon-Journal* to the *York (Pennsylvania) Daily Record* and including most of the nation's large dailies in between. Television accounted for 18.4 percent of MRS inquiries, including the major commercial networks and PBS. Press services and free-lance writers made 16.6 percent of the inquiries; magazines 14.2 percent and radio 9.3.

Inquiries with a local slant outnumbered inquiries with a nationwide focus by 67.3 percent to 32.7 percent.

What do the journalists want to know? A sampling of topics from 1983-84 tells the story: how toy guns affect behavior; current AIDS research; dioxin; treatment of zoo animals; high technology venture capital.

When a journalist gets a breaking story with a short deadline, as Dave Pearlman, science editor of the *San Francisco Chronicle*, did in late January 1984, finding reliable resources quickly can be a problem. Pearlman called the MRS at 3:10 P.M., Eastern time, that day to ask for the name of a scientist who could discuss the effect on public health of EDB (ethylene dibromide), long used as a crop pesticide but recently identified as a possible cause of cancer in laboratory rats and mice. Pearlman wanted to know if traces of EDB found in packaged cake mixes could be toxic.

The MRS ran a search of its computer file and came up with four names. It first called Dr. Perrie Adams, director of the Behavioral Toxicology Laboratory of the University of Texas' medical branch. As it does when calling any scientist about a media inquiry, the MRS asked Dr. Adams if this was a subject he would be prepared to discuss. He was, having conducted recent laboratory tests involving EDB and rats. At 3:30, just 20 minutes after Pearlman had called, the MRS called him back and gave him Dr. Adams' name and telephone number.

Forty minutes after that, the MRS had canvassed the other three scientists—a pharmacologist, a toxologist and a professor of environmental medicine—and gave their names and telephone numbers to Pearlman. Pearlman contacted two of the four experts, and the next morning a detailed background article on EDB appeared in the *Chronicle*.

For its services the MRS does not charge journalists or their organizations. Instead, tax-deductible gifts from media companies make up 10 percent of the service's annual budget. Corporations give another 10 percent and foundations make up the balance, 80 percent.

FACS—BRINGING JOURNALISTS AND BUSINESS TOGETHER

The founders of the Foundation for American Communications (FACs) set out in 1975 to create neither a media watchdog not a clearinghouse of information. Their objective, according to president Jack Cox, was "to help improve the information seen by the public about business and the economy."[130]

Now, hundreds of business-media conferences, training sessions and publications later, FACs considers itself a success and is taken seriously both by the corporate world and major media organizations.

FACs does most of its work through conferences; however, it also provides media training. It emphasizes that the latter work is heavily oriented to print media, whereas most media training specialists concentrate on the electronic media, especially television, and platform appearances.

Typically, FACs will organize a conference for business and media participants, with panelists from both categories. One such, the Western Conference on Business & Media in April 1982, was jointly sponsored by Columbia University, the *Los Angeles Times* and the *Long Beach (California) Press-Telegram*. It was held in Long Beach.

In January 1985, FACs organized a conference on Central America under the sponsorship of the *Los Angeles Times*. The 100-person conference, held in San Diego, included a variety of speakers—Assistant Secretary of State Langhorne Motley, the finance minister of Mexico, a leading Nicaraguan journalist and guerrilla leaders from both the right and left, from Nicaragua and El Salvador, respectively.

"We want to help business executives improve their understanding of how the news process works," says Cox, once an aide to former Rep. Barry Goldwater, Jr. "We set out to demystify people about the media by bringing business and media people together."[131]

FACs, which is a not-for-profit foundation, has provided precrisis media training for corporations such as the Six Flags theme park chain. Large financial organizations, such as Citibank, have put "hundreds of senior executives through our media orientation," says Cox. At events put on for corporate executives, FACs brings in journalists as guest speakers to help the conferees better understand the workings and role of the media.

Trade associations have also used FACs media conferences for their members. One recent conference, sponsored by the Aerospace Industries Association, used a real case history (about alleged cost overruns on production of the C5B airplane), with the cooperation of Lockheed, manufacturers of the aircraft, NBC and the *Los Angeles Times*. In this case, according to Cox, a "public interest" group had fed information from a Government Accounting Office report to the media in a way that was incorrect. The conference speakers went over the steps that all parties took to get correct information to the public.

FACs also claims to be the largest supplier of "media education" to nonprofit, eleemosynary organizations. The Gannett Foundation has provided a grant to FACs for conducting these seminars for the nonprofits. During 1985 there will be 45 seminars for community leaders doing voluntary work for the nonprofits.

At its all-journalist conferences, FACs wants to "help the journalists better understand the economy and business, and we do it in a nonideological way," Cox says.[132] The format for these conferences is to have 40 journalists sit at a U-shaped table. There are also "observers" and speakers on economics and business. The tone is informal and conversational.

Since 1979, when FACs conducted its first journalists' conference, there have been 63, of which 53 focused on business and the economy.

Usually, these conferences are open to any individual journalist, who pays a $50 entry fee for the two-and-a-half day event. The conferences are subsidized by grants from foundations and media companies. Cox emphasizes that no government or corporation funds are involved in the journalists' conferences.

FACs also conducts programs for individual news organizations, such as NBC, aimed at executives of its owned-and-operated stations and its affiliates.

A recent Ford Foundation grant will enable FACs to conduct a two-year study of business and economics reporting by the news media and to develop recommendations on how best to raise the level of reporting.

FACs relies heavily on foundation contributions to underwrite its budget. It has approximately 120 contributors. A majority of its support—65 percent—comes from foundations and media organizations. The rest comes from the general business world.

Along with its conferences and media training programs, FACs publishes concise primers on media relations. One is designed primarily for eleemosynary organizations, another for business executives. Both are titled, "Who..What..When..Where..Why.. How to Tell Your Story." These guides, at $3.95 and $5.00, respectively, are available from the Foundation for American Communications (FACs), 3383 Barham Boulevard, Los Angeles, California 90068.

NJC—STARTING WITH STUDENTS

FACs was not the only media education organization to begin life in 1975. The National Journalism Center was founded in Washington, D.C. the same year. A unit of the nonprofit Education & Research Institute, the NJC has been training prospective journalists ever since, "within a context of traditional values," according to M. Stanton Evans, chairman of E&RI. Evans, former editor of the *Indianapolis Star* and a prominent conservative columnist and commentator, conducts three NJC 12-week sessions each year, in the spring, summer and fall. Most of the interns in the program are college students. The NJC helps to place them in media jobs on completion of their training. In 1984, the NJC trained some 80 aspiring journalists, selected from more than 500 applicants.

In a letter to E&RI supporters in December 1984, Evans noted that more than 200 NJC alumni are now working in mainstream media and at related jobs for the *Wall Street Journal*, the Evans & Novak syndicated column, *Harper's*, C-SPAN, "NBC Nightly News," Gannett News Service, the *Detroit News*, the *San Diego Union*, *Congressional Quarterly*, the A.P. and U.P.I, and The Voice of America.

During their 12-week training in Washington, each intern spends the first six weeks doing research for and writing a paper on a public policy issue. For the second six weeks, each works with a newspaper, magazine, news service, syndicated columnist or public organization. Added to this program is a menu of seminars featuring media people and policy makers.

If, as an E&RI newsletter states, the National Journalism Center is "aimed at restoring balance to the media," its slow but steady growth is an encouraging sign. For the business executive worried about one day being interviewed by one of those more-radical-than-their-elders journalism school students survey by Lichter and Rothman (see Chapter Two), there may be comfort in the fact that NJC graduates are becoming more numerous every year, thus providing something of a counterweight. Evans, in a *Washington Times* interview in June 1984, put his goal plainly: "Our modest objective, and we are under no illusions that we are going to have immediate impact, is to try to get some people into the media who are not liberals."

Postscript:
The Ethics Perplexity

That America has come off the Media High with a crash there seems no doubt. As *Christian Science Monitor* columnist Melvin Maddocks states, the readers of journalists these days "are cheering for almost anybody who, for almost any reason, sues them."[133]

Journalists, always a skeptical lot, deepened their skepticism in the wake of the Vietnam war and Watergate, and they broadened it to cover virtually every institution in our society. The public, finding its traditional authority figures and heroes with feet of clay, followed suit and found the only heroes left were journalists.

This situation, in turn, seemed to spawn a generation of politicians determined to create a risk-free world; and what followed was a barrage of laws and regulations that had the effect of hamstringing many of society's traditional institutions, such as business, the military and the criminal justice system.

From the late sixties until the early eighties, the nation's news media luxuriated in the self-appointed role of Great Arbiter of Accountability. The media demanded accountability of everyone, it seemed, except their own practitioners. In time, frustration with media self-righteousness spread, first among certain businesses and industries that came under what appeared to be guilty-till-proven-innocent media attacks; later to nearly everyone in American society. Perhaps the almost universal frustration with the media was a result of the inability of the media to explain our complex world adequately. Or perhaps it was caused by the maddening tendency of the media to oversimplify everything in an effort to "squeeze a day's history into a footnote; a day's reflection into a one-liner" (as columnist Maddocks put it).

The evidence of disenchantment with the media began piling up in the early eighties. A Pulitzer prize was returned because the reporter invented the central figure in the winning story; a veteran writer for a prestigious magazine confessed to having rearranged people and places in his stories for two decades; a freelance writer did an "eyewitness" account of horrible conditions in Cambodia from the comfort of his home, and plagiarized part of the story to boot; a jury found that *Time* defamed Israeli Gen. Ariel Sharon and printed falsehoods about him (although the jury acquitted the magazine of "malice"); Gen. Westmoreland sued CBS for a record amount; a *Wall Street Journal* reporter was tried in federal court and convicted for feeding market tips to friends who profited handsomely from them; North Carolina's Sen. Jesse Helms mounted a nationwide campaign among conservatives to take control of CBS; the Mobil Corporation announced that it had been mistreated by the *Wall Street Journal* once too often, withdrew its advertising and said that it would refuse to talk with *Journal* reporters in the future.

While these events are not connected, the pattern is clear. And the news media are worried. Each new major libel suit seems to bring a rush of introspective columns, op-ed page articles, and editorials about media responsibility, ethics and, of course, the hallowed First Amendment to the Constitution.

In 1984, *USA Today* devoted its entire editorial page twice to media questions. One was on "Media Fairness," the other on "Journalism Ethics."

In an article in the latter, Richard V. Allen, former presidential national security adviser, suggested four remedies to what he called "ambush journalism":

1. Establish "unequivocal standards of conduct" to make sure that reporting is fair.
2. Mandate that corrections and retractions appear on p. 1 or at the beginning of a newscast, running the same length as the charges.
3. Improve media access for people "who have been wrongly attacked and accused." In the case of television, Allen says, the person attacked should be allowed to appear live and to confront the reporter who initiated the story.
4. "Require reporters and editors...working on government affairs to file financial disclosure statements as complete as those required of public officials." Allen proposes publication of these statements, too. Jody Powell, White House press secretary in the Carter administration, supports this concept in his book, *The Other Side of the Story.*

Each of these proposals will find its supporters and, if a simple way could be found to implement them, might enjoy great popularity. The trouble is that, with the possible exception of the last one, they cannot be implemented without the creation of a new quasi-judicial bureaucracy or the imposition of government dictation of newspaper and newscast composition, or both. In short, the remedies might be a lot worse than the transgressions that brought them about.

Allen himself was a victim of herd instinct journalism (as discussed in Chapter 8; pp. 82-85) and has good reason to be upset.

He did take vigorous countermeasures, however, and this still remains the best way to deal with the situation. Institutionalizing remedies will almost certainly result in tangled legal interpretations. Besides, rather than deliberate distortions or vendettas, according to *Washington Post* columnist Robert J. Samuelson, "the press's most offensive characteristic is its obsessive self-righteousness, which can border on nastiness."[134]

In addition to waving the First Amendment at every sign of criticism—something that probably inflames its adversaries all the more—journalism is responding in new and more fundamental ways. In 1984, "reacting to the eroding credibility of the press," 13 of the nation's university-level schools of journalism added ethics courses for the first time.[135] These courses were added to the 22 that had been started between 1981 and 1983. By the end of 1984, 40 percent of the nation's journalism schools were offering ethics courses. Seven years before, in 1977, the figure was only 27 percent.

Renewed emphasis on ethics, and rigorous thinking about moral dilemmas on the part of journalism students should help produce more journalists who temper their idealism with a willingness to understand that there is more than one point of view on an issue. This, alone, won't cure the problem, but then neither will a set of federally mandated ethics rules.

Keeping the news media fair and honest is a matter requiring vigilance and constant attention. If you have visited a country where the media are government-controlled, you have experienced the realization that you would not want ours to be anything but free—as fractious, irritating and imperfect as they are.

The best guarantee of both a free and a fair press (and electronic media) is steady interaction between the media and their critics—frequently, you and me. If the media are wrong, talk back. Take vigorous countermeasures if you think these are necessary to right a wrong. Even sue, if need be. If the medium's owning company is publicly traded, threaten a corporate takeover if necessary and if you think (as U.S. Sen. Jesse Helms apparently does in his effort to take over CBS) that this will make that media organization more careful in the development and checking of stories.

Do whatever is necessary to keep the media from feeling infallible and invulnerable. Neither they—nor we—are gods, and the constant reminder that all of us are human and that we have responsibilities is the best insurance that the media will serve a useful, positive role in the long run.

Footnotes

Chapter 1:

1. On Sunday, June 18, 1972 an article about the incident, carrying Bernstein's byline, appeared in the *Post*.

2. *Washington Post*, April 6, 1976.

3. *Political Animal*, October 23, 1981.

4. *Aim Report*, November 1983.

5. From Proceedings of "The Press: Free & Responsible?" symposium, University of Texas, April 3, 1981.

6. "John Lofton's Journal," *Washington Times*, December 16, 1983.

7. *National Journal*, February 4, 1984.

8. *"Journalism Under Fire," Time*, December 12, 1983.

9. Ibid.

10. Quoted in *USA Today*, December 15, 1983.

11. *New York Times*, April 19, 1981.

12. *Washington Post*, April 19, 1981.

13. Quoted by Jonathan Friendly, *New York Times*, November 15, 1981.

14. U.S. District Court Judge Charles L. Brieant, in *Reliance Insurance Company v. Barrons*, 1977.

15. "Journalism Under Fire," *Time*, December 12, 1983.

Chapter 2:

16. Until the rise of objective reporting during the last third of the 19th century, much reporting was tendentious. And the muckrakers of the turn of the century were certainly practicing advocacy journalism. In this book, the term refers to latter-day use of the form.

17. *New York Times*, June 19, 1984.

18. Ibid.

19. *Washington Post* , November 8, 1983.

20. *Lou Cannon, Reporting*, Sacramento, California Journal Press, 1977, p. 5.

21. Ibid., pp. 8, 9.

22. Ibid., p. 12.

23. Ibid., p. 31.

24. *Broadcasting*, January 1984.

25. *The Baron Report*, February 13, 1984.

26. The Lichter-Rothman media study was conducted under the auspices of the Research Institute on International Change at Columbia University. This, and a survey by the authors of business leaders, was supervised by Research Analysis, a survey research firm. The findings were published in *Public Opinion*, a journal of the American Enterprise Institute for Public Policy Research, Washington, D.C., November 1981.

27. $27,620 (1982). Source: Office of Policy Information, The White House, March 2, 1984.

28. *Los Angeles Times*, October 26, 1983.

29. From Linda Lichter, Robert Lichter and Stanley Rothman, "The Once and Future Journalists," *Washington Journalism Review*, December 1982.

30. Ibid.

31. Ibid.

32. Interview in the *Washington Times*, August 5, 1983.

33. *New York Post*, October 25, 1983.

34. *Washington Post*, July 13, 1983.

35. Cannon, op. cit., p. 19.

36. Ibid., p. 48.

37. Michael J. Robinson, "Media, Rate Thyselves," *Washington Journalism Review*, December 1983.

38. Ibid.

39. Ibid.

40. Address to Gannett News Service executives, December 13, 1983.

41. Ibid.

42. Ibid.

43. "The Speaker and the Listener: a Public Perspective on Freedom of Expression," The Public Agenda Foundation, 1980.

44. Ibid., p. 20.

45. Ibid., p. 25.

Chapter 3:

46. "Inside the Power House," *Washington Post*, June 28, 1984.

47. *Los Angeles Times*, June 24, 1984.

48. "How Coors Won Friends and Influenced '60 Minutes,'" *Denver Post*, Empire Magazine, October 16, 1983.

49. Ibid.

50. Ibid.

51. Ibid.

Chapter 4:

52. *Trends in Attitudes Toward Television and Other Media*: A Twenty-four Year Review, a report by the Roper Organization, Inc., was published by the Television Information Office, New York, in April 1983.

53. Marshall McLuhan, *Understanding Media*, New York, McGraw-Hill Book Company, 1964, p. 22.

54. Ibid., p. 23.

55. Rudy Maxa, "How to Stand Out in a Crowd," *Washingtonian*, April 1984.

56. Ibid.

57. McLuhan, op. cit., p. 317.

58. Interview with the author, February 1, 1984.

59. Ibid.

60. Quoted in the *New York Times*, July 7, 1983.

61. Holmes M. Brown, "How TV Reported the Recovery," *The Wall Street Journal*, March 6, 1984.

62. Ibid.

63. Interview with the author, April 24, 1984.

64. Interview on "60 Minutes," January 1, 1984.

65. Congressional Quarterly, May 5, 1984.

66. Ibid.

67. Interview on "60 Minutes," January 1, 1984.

68. Ibid.

69. "How Coors Won Friends and Influenced '60 Minutes,'" *Denver Post, Empire Magazine*, October 15, 1983.

70. Ibid.

71. Ibid.

Chapter 5:

72. "Future Trends in Broadcast Journalism," survey conducted by Frank N. Magid Associates, Inc., August 1984.

Chapter 6:

73. "Relating to the Readers in the '80s," survey conducted by Clark Martire & Bartolomeo, Inc. for the American Society of Newspaper Editors, May 1984.

74. Ibid., p. 9.

Chapter 7:

75. "Journalism Under Fire," *Time*, December 12, 1983.

Chapter 8:

76. *USA Today*, April 5, 1983.

77. *Wall Street Journal*, September 3, 1981.

78. Jonathan Z. Larsen, "The Battle of Black Rock," *New York*, October 24, 1983.

79. Ibid., p. 43.

80. Ibid., p. 45.

81. *Washington Journalism Review*, May 1984.

82. *Washington Post*, January 15, 1984.

Chapter 9:

83. Interview with the author, February 15, 1984.

84. "Lessons from a Hot Dog Maker's Ordeal," *Fortune*, March 7, 1983.

85. Ibid.

86. Ibid.

87. Interview with the author, February 15, 1984.

88. Ibid.

89. Ibid.

90. Ibid.

91. Interview with the author, March 25, 1983. (Name withheld at request of the source.)

92. Interview with the author, January 5, 1984.

93. Herbert Schmertz, "Advocacy Has its Rewards," *Communicator's Journal*, May/June 1983.

94. Interview with the author, January 5, 1984.

95. Ibid.

96. "Turning Off the Lights," *Forbes*, November 7, 1983.

97. Ibid.

Chapter 10:

98. "The News Council—What Did It In?" *Columbia Journalism Review*, May 1984.

99. Interview with the author, November 3, 1983.

100. "National News Council Will Dissolve," *New York Times*, March 23, 1984.

101.   Interview with the author, November 3, 1983.

102.   Interview in *The Retired Officer*, August 1981.

103.   Interview with the author, September 15, 1983.

104.   Ibid.

105.   Ibid.

106.   Ibid.

107.   Ibid.

108.   Ibid.

109.   Ibid.

110.   "What Do Ombudsmen Do?" *Columbia Journalism Review*, May 1984.

111.   Ibid.

112.   Ibid.

113.   Interview with the author, November 7, 1983.

114.   "What Do Ombudsmen Do?" *Columbia Journalism Review*, May 1984.

115.   Interview with the author, November 7, 1983.

116.   Ibid.

117.   Ibid.

118.   Interview in *Time*, quoted in *Forbes*, July 18, 1983, p. 18.

119.   "The Ombudsmen's Story," *Washington Journalism Review*, May 1984.

120.   Interview with the author, November 7, 1983.

121. Interview with the author, May 1, 1984.

122. Ibid.

123. Ibid.

124. Ibid.

125. Ibid.

126. Ibid.

Chapter 11:

127. "When 'Sixty Minutes' Comes Knocking," *Frequent Flyer*, July 1984.

128. *Jack O'Dwyer's Newsletter*, March 21, 1984.

129. Media Resource Service, 1983-84 report.

130. Interview with the author, January 15, 1985.

131. Ibid.

132. Ibid.

Postscript:

133. *Christian Science Monitor*, January 23, 1985.

134. *Washington Post*, January 2, 1985.

135. *Washington Times*, December 1984.

Index

INDEX